Second Corinthians

A New Testament Commentary

Keith Trump

Second Corinthians: A New Testament Commentary

ISBN: 978-168031-070-2
© 2016 by Trump of God Ministries
Carmel, IN

Published by Harrison House Publishers
Tulsa, OK 74155
www.harrisonhouse.com

19 18 17 16 10 9 8 7 6 5 4 3 2 1

Author photo (on back) by Halleigh Castino
Printed in the United States of America.

To Lori:
γυνή ἀδελφιδός μου

Table of Contents

Foreword

When I think of Keith Trump and the Greek language, I picture a kid in a candy store. Not that there's anything immature about Keith or his approach to the language of the New Testament, but his absolute delight, exuberance, and enthusiasm is readily apparent. Keith loves the Greek New Testament and has an intense passion to help non-academics benefit from the rich insights provided by the language in which Paul wrote.

Keith's *New Testament Commentary on Second Corinthians* will serve as a tremendously beneficial resource to ministers and laymen alike. This work provides great contextual information, both historically and linguistically. For readers, it helps create a three-dimensional, living-color perspective of this epistle: the time in which it was written, Paul's intent in writing it, and the vital nuances of this message to the Corinthians.

I can't think of a better person to learn from than Keith Trump. He has a solid academic track record, and a consistent history of effective ministry with a view toward practical application. I have rarely met anyone as eager to help other people "get it" when it comes to the basics of Scripture, and he is well qualified to help take people into deeper, more profound biblical insights.

Finally, Keith has a unique ability to take what could be perceived as daunting or overwhelming information and simplify it for the benefit of basic students. What you will find in this excellent work is not an isolated, ivory-tower academic trying to impress you with barely intelligible information, but a caring pastor helping to feed believers with the richness of God's Word.

Reverend Tony C. Cooke
Author and Bible Teacher

About the Translation and Transliteration

The translation of 2 Corinthians contained in this commentary resulted from a careful consultation with Greek texts. Readers will not find in this book a mere cut, paste, and amalgamation of several pre-existing English versions. After diving deep into Greek manuscripts, recording word for word equivalents, and couching meaning (without losing richness in modern English), I resurfaced with a document filled with the unchanging life of God which so drastically changes our lives. Out of respect for both readers and the current community of New Testament scholars, I have also compared my findings against today's well-respected English translations. In this translation's pages, the downcast will find colossal comfort, the broken will grasp heroic healing, the condemned will acquire real release, and the complacent will witness the shattering of every excuse for wallowing in mediocrity.

The transliteration (attempting to employ English letters corresponding with Greek characters), although necessary at times, can prove a bit confusing. For example, the Greek preposition σύν transliterates as "sun." In no way does the English term "sun" convey the same meaning as σύν. Rather than a reference to the star of our solar system, this particular preposition signifies something "gathered together for a unified purpose." In English, it actually comes over as the prefix *syn*. For example, the "synoptic" Gospels represent three distinct, yet exceptionally unified (syn) viewpoints (optics) of the life and teachings of Jesus. Similarly, a "synagogue" signifies a group of people gathered together (syn) from all over a city to a distinct location to learn about the (agogue) ways of life in God. Nevertheless, standard transliteration requires that particular form.

Further cloudiness often arises when Greek endings come into play. The Greek language embeds, in the end of words, particular codes signifying a term's specific function and number. Thus, Greek words have both a basic meaning encapsulated in a term's root and further information contained in its ending.

The same thing, although not nearly as complex, occurs in English grammar. For example, the word "cars" signifies both the root meaning found in "car" and the concept of plural seen in the ending "s." In Greek, a word can look as many as twenty different ways depending on its ending. For example, in 2 Corinthians 1:4, Paul uses the term translated "comfort" four times in a single verse. However, the Greek word has a different ending for each particular occurrence: (παρακαλῶν) (παρακαλεῖν) (παρακλήσεως) (παρακαλούμεθα). In each instance, the first six or seven letters display similarity while the last few letters differ. This results from the consistency of the word's root (meaning comfort) and the dissimilarity of the various endings. Those possessing a knowledge of Greek can both quickly spot the differences and accurately discern the meaning couched in the endings.

What about those not well versed in Greek? Thankfully, lexicons (Greek dictionaries) list words in their most basic form. Those not proficient in Greek need only to know the term's most basic form along with its transliteration. In order to guide readers through the grammatical maze, this commentary presents transliterated words in the forms found while using a lexicon. In the case of the Greek term for "comfort," one would find παρακαλέω (parakaleo). Armed with this knowledge, one can then look the word up in a lexicon to discover a startlingly greater depth of meaning.

Introduction

The current American residential landscape lies littered with a sea of cookie cutter, bland, vinyl clad boxes hilariously marketed as custom homes. These structures require a relatively miniscule investment of money, time, and creativity. Developers cast aside quality materials, careful planning, and real artistry in favor of cheap, rapid, and easy construction. Like the rabid consumption of fast food, a powerful sense of regret often seizes buyers of such homes. After a few minutes, physical malaise causes one to ask, "Why did I eat this junk food?" Similarly, after a few years, molded siding, sagging roofs, and shifted foundations confront homeowners with the unavoidable question: "Why did I buy this piece of junk?" Conversely, the building of highly functional, immensely beautiful, and timeless homes requires an extensive outlay of treasure, talent, and time.

The same axiomatic principle applies to theological works. This law functions universally because God built it into His universe. Today's field of commentaries has become overgrown with weeds masquerading as substantial books. The church — particularly its camps labeled "full-Gospel," "charismatic," "word of faith," and "prophetic" — has, while enjoying many great moves of God, experienced a baptism in theological drivel. Yet, within the Spirit-filled streams of Christianity exists a remnant voraciously hungry for substantive revelation. I have witnessed this phenomenon on the rare occasion when a well-written, scripturally-grounded book appears in these circles of Christianity. For example, when Rick Renner released his *Light in the Darkness*, it flooded the desert of pop churchianity with living water.

Through thirty years of hands-on ministry and nearly twenty years of intense studies in Hebrew, Aramaic, and Greek, the Lord has prepared me for producing this commentary series. During this time of traveling ministry, church planting, pastoring, writing, and language studies, Jesus poured into me for the purpose of pouring back into His church. This commentary springs, not from a self-centered conception in my mind, but from a direct commission in my spirit.

Two years ago, I began assembling a fifteen-week-long seminar on church history. During this time of preparation, I entered into a season of intense prayer. While praying in the Spirit one day, the Lord began speaking to me regarding the reformers who had translated Scripture out of Latin and into the languages of the people. Having the Bible in their own language transformed massive segments of the body of Christ. God then told me, "I called them [men who had translated Scripture into native languages] to get my word into the language of the people. I am calling you to get my people into the language of my Word [Hebrew, Aramaic, and Greek]. You will go around the world imparting this revelation to the church. Now, go and do it!" Out of obedience to this command, the Getting Greek seminars, Handling Hebrew seminars, Roots church history seminars, and this commentary series sprang. The Head of the church intensely desires to get his body out of the shallows and swimming in the deep end of his revelatory pool.

I designed this series in a manner to avoid four pitfalls many commentaries drop into. To begin, some come weighted down with a level of academic material appreciated by a fantastically small quotient of readers. The larger audience grows either quickly disinterested or indefinitely lost in the minutia of an endless catalogue of sources. Although scholarly sound, after the first chapter the work grows so boring that its remaining pages could be left blank to save on costs. While intelligent readers appreciate a meaty bibliography, an overwhelming banter of "scholar x says this and scholar y says that" looks more like rabbinic Rabbah than a serious commentary. Books structured thusly spend countless pages painstakingly answering questions no one is asking. Even the most competent scholarship proves unhelpful if, with all its potential to provide bread, it offers a stone instead. While trained scholars will garner helpful insights from this form of writing, God never intended for his Word to remain under the guardianship of initiatic theologians.

Therefore, while this commentary regularly discusses matters of Greek grammar and vocabulary, readers completely unfamiliar with biblical languages can still greatly benefit from its content. Although it includes well-researched details about cultural nuances affecting the text, it refuses to mire down its audience. The commentary arrests its readers' attention, takes them by the hand, and leads them into the very center of Corinthian life. But it does not leave them there. It captures the acts of God occurring in the lives of particular first-century Christians and applies them to every believer alive today.

Other commentaries serve to simply repeat the Scriptures they propose to expound upon. While the motive to deal with every single verse proves noble, some passages require little comment. This shows itself most glaringly in verses wherein a truth has already received treatment earlier in the same commentary. For example, in one chapter, the text may read, "I took Titus and went to Corinth." Then, much later in the same book, a nearly identical phrase occurs. If the commentator has already elaborated on both the character of Titus and the setting of Corinth, no real need exists to explicate an identical twin of the previous sentence. Filling out the book's page count may indeed make the work appear overflowing with a bounty of revelation. However, astute readers quickly realize that such works, although lengthy, remain full of theologically empty calories. The same thing occurs in public speech: length does not automatically equate to power. Preachers often speak a great truth within the first five minutes of a message, repeat that truth a second time, and belabor it for an additional hour.

In response, this commentary allocates its chief focus on the major passages within a given chapter. Out of respect for the preciousness of time, it never majors on the minors.

The third mistake found in commentaries stems from commentators who widely overstep their knowledge. I have personally seen well-known preachers put forth Greek — and at times Hebrew — word studies that prove laughable at best and heretical at worst. Throwing down Greek words in order to prop up popular theological presuppositions has become a favorite tactic of many preachers. While far more common in sermons, commentaries are not immune from such spurious tactics. This dirty water usually flows from those with little or no training in biblical languages.

Sadly, most employing this method hide their lack of Greek language skills under the cloak of "super pastor," and people blindly swallow arguments based on a grave mishandling of Greek vocabulary. After all, anyone leading a large scale ministry "must know what he is talking about." While such leaders may possess a passel of legitimate giftings, a true understanding of Greek does not automatically come as a standard pastoral accessory; knowing how to use *Strong's Concordance* remains a far cry from a thorough grasp of Greek. Far too often, Christian celebrities pass off major theological assumptions based on computer software at best and third-hand information at worst. Thus, eminence in one realm (preaching or organization leadership) produces blindness to incompetence in another (language skills).

Dexterous manipulation of words make it possible to force theological presuppositions into doctrinal statements. This, however, amounts to pushing the Bible through a mold of personal bias rather than allowing God's word to mold theology. The church needs, not a god made in our image, but the Spirit's work transforming us into His image.

The Greek translation and content contained in this commentary remains rooted and grounded in Scripture, considers hundreds of years of former scholarship, and is relative to current day application. In a few cases, I do differ from conventional opinion on Greek grammatical matters. However, regarding such differences, I stand quite prepared to provide a satisfactory explanation to those competent to form a cogent judgment.

The final snare commentaries often fall into regards an obsession with application. This form of error stands on the opposite end of the spectrum from the first trap mentioned above. While relentlessly -academic works suffer from a near absence of life application, those in this subterfuge voraciously lend themselves to personal utilization at the expense of truth. Incorrect exegesis gives birth to tainted doctrine. Tainted doctrine produces aberrant belief. Aberrant belief fosters an unscriptural course of life. Thus application based on inaccurate interpretation, no matter how well-meaning, miserably fails to advance the Kingdom of God. In an age when most weigh Scripture in the balance of their personal experiences rather than vice versa, many eagerly bite this deceptive bait.

Without question, the "gospel does not reach a full expression with mere words, but also includes demonstrations of the Spirit's power" (1 Cor. 2:4). However, all Old and New Covenant writers filtered any demonstrations of power through the written Word. Therefore, this commentary seeks to anchor all application, no matter how lofty, deep within the fertile ground of God's Word. By abiding in the vine growing from that soil, believers will bear, not here-today-and-gone-tomorrow fads, but a bumper crop of everlasting fruit.

Authorship

Although "few pieces of correspondence by St. Paul have attracted so much controversial comment as has 2 Corinthians,"[1] its Pauline authorship remains largely uncontested.[2] Several internal factors point to the apostle Paul as author. First, a pseudo-author would obviously portray Paul as soaring rather than suffering. Furthermore, in the plot structure of 2 Corinthians, Paul often takes a strong defensive posture. An imposter would likely have structured the epistle in a more melodramatic fashion.

In addition, on several points, the author takes his cues from life situations known only to himself and his original audience. Indeed, the epistle "often reads like a one-sided telephone conversation." [3] Any mountebank worth his salt would not have presented a letter so full of seeming obscurity.[4]

Although Pauline style and vocabulary can be seen in 2 Corinthians, one should not be too quick to pin down Paul's exact style. In many instances, Paul wrote his letters by means of a scribe. Obviously, in some measure, the style of the particular scribe found its way into Paul's letters. Furthermore, due to the episode-driven nature of his letters, his style is extremely fluid. For these reasons, "the style of Paul, like his theology, has challenged the attention of the greatest minds."[5]

Although his style often changes to fit the situation at hand,[6] Paul's "passionate pastoral concern for all the churches"[7] remains a constant in his letters. This unmistakable character trait of Paul serves as the strongest internal evidence for his authorship of this letter. Without a doubt, Paul's pastoral heart (as seen in other Pauline letters) beats in nearly every major section of 2 Corinthians.[8]

Finally, in 2 Corinthians 1:1 and 10:1, the text itself stoutly identifies Paul as its author. The sum of internal evidence clearly points to Paul as author and throws the burden of proof on those who would argue otherwise.

The overall validity of this letter is further attested by credible, external evidence. Although apparently unknown to Clement of Rome, the epistle is alluded to in the letters of Barnabas and Diognetus.

Furthermore, various quotations from 2 Corinthians appear in the writings of Polycarp, Irenaeus, Clement of Alexandria, Tertullian, and Cyprian. It is also noteworthy that the epistle gained entrance into both the Marcion and Muratorian canons. Finally, men such as Athenagoius and Theophilus of Antioch also displayed obvious familiarity with 2 Corinthians.[9]

Date, Location, and Occasion

Much of the information concerning the date and place of 2 Corinthians comes from the book of Acts. In fact, apart from Paul's autobiographic references, the chief source for information about his Corinthian connection is the book of Acts.[10] The date of Paul's arrival in Corinth can be substantiated by the mention in Acts 18:12 of the Roman proconsulship of Lucius Junius Gallio Annaeus. According to a reliable inscription, Gallio was proconsul in Corinth from AD. 51–52[11] or AD 52–53.[12] Luke explains that Paul first arrived in Corinth during his second missionary journey (detailed in Acts 15:36–18:22). Sometime during his eighteen month (18:11) stay, certain angry Jews brought Paul before Gallio (18:12) who immediately dismissed the case. Following his encounter with Gallio, Paul remained in Corinth for an undisclosed amount of time.

After departing Corinth, Paul stopped briefly in Ephesus (18:19–20) before moving on to Caesarea and ultimately the church in Jerusalem (18:22). Next, he traveled to the "original sending church" at Antioch[13] (18:23, cf. 13:13–14:24) and stayed there for "some time," before launching his third missionary journey (18:23). After passing briefly through Galatia and Phrygia, Paul settles in Ephesus for two and a half to three years (19:8, 10; 20:31).

Once settled in Ephesus, Paul's ministry was punctuated by periodic communications (in the form of letters and by delegation) to and from Corinth that exposed "the emerging problems in that community and between that community and Paul."[14] Thankfully, the two surviving (1 and 2 Corinthians) letters provide the modern reader with inside information regarding these events. Unfortunately, the other letters from Paul to Corinth and none of the letters from the Corinthians to Paul exist today.

Although both 1 and 2 Corinthians provide building blocks for a reconstruction of events, there are certainly historical gaps in the record.[15] However, by bridging these gaps in gestalt like fashion, one can produce an account that is at least plausible. In other words, from the documents of Acts and the Corinthian epistles, it is possible to make a "tentative"[16] or "rough outline of Paul's activities at Corinth and his correspondence with the Christians in that city." First Corinthians 5:9 mentions his "previous letter," which he wrote sometime between 53 and 54 AD. Although many details regarding this letter remain uncertain, we know that Paul strongly exhorted the Corinthians to avoid fellowship with (sexually) immoral believers. Apparently the Corinthians took his advice to an unscriptural extreme by distancing themselves from society as a whole.[17]

Next, between 53 and 55 AD, a delegation for Corinth arrived (1:11, 16:17) to inquire about a variety of topics including divisions in the church, sexual relations, local temple worship, food offered to idols, spiritual gifts, and the collection for the Jerusalem church. In response to this inquiry (perhaps in the spring of AD 55) Paul penned the epistle of 1 Corinthians.[18] Next, he commissioned Timothy to accomplish a twofold task. First, he was to deliver and explain the letter of 1 Corinthians. Second, he was to return to Paul with a kind of spiritual progress report concerning the Corinthian church (16:11–12).

Unfortunately, Timothy (or some other messenger)[19] brought back a poignantly negative report. The news that the Corinthians had rejected his recent letter (1 Corinthians) prompted Paul to make a hasty and "painful" visit in AD 55 (2 Cor. 2:1). Upon his arrival, Paul found the situation grim indeed. Apparently the Corinthians had allowed false apostles into their midst who encouraged the church to reject both the apostleship and instruction of Paul. He left town after a rather unpleasant confrontation with the church.

Next, he returned to Ephesus and realized that, under the circumstances, a return visit in the near future could create more grief for them as well as for himself (2:1–2, 1:6). Instead, in late AD 55, Paul wrote and Titus delivered a "severe" or "tearful" letter (2:3–4, 7:8–12, 8:6). In late AD 55 or early 56, Paul went to Troas and waited for any news from Titus. For Paul, in this case, no news was bad news. For one reason or another — Paul most plausibly figured that the Corinthians had rejected Titus — Titus never arrived in Troas (2 Cor. 12–13).

After experiencing a no-show in Troas, Paul traveled to Macedonia (in mid-late AD 56) where, to his delight, Titus greeted him with good news. Many in the Corinthian church had responded positively (with repentance) to the "tearful letter" (7:6–16). However, not all the Corinthians had warmed up to Paul's sorrowful epistle. Tragically, some in the church still openly challenged his credibility.

Sometime in mid to late AD 56, in response to this mixture of good and bad news, Paul sat down in Macedonia (possibly Philippi)[20] and wrote the first nine chapters of 2 Corinthians. After hearing news of a fresh attack by the super apostles,[21] Paul wrote the remaining chapters of the epistle.

In short, 2 Corinthians was not produced in a vacuum. Instead, each event mentioned above played an intricate part in forming a framework for the epistle. During the entire course of Paul's relationship with the Corinthians, the influx of the false apostles was "by far the most serious problem."[22] The question of their identity has been called "one of the crucial questions for the understanding of the New Testament and the origins of Christianity."[23]

One should exercise care when reconstructing Paul's opponents. Readers must always keep in mind the nagging reality that "we are privy to only one side of the dialogue."[24] Some argue that the opponents were patent Gnostics. Others contend that these false apostles were textbook Judaizers.[25] Yet the idea that one must classify the opponents as either Judaizers or Gnostics presents a false dilemma. Although the opponents were clearly Jewish ("Hebrews," "Israelites," and "the seed of Abraham" cf. 11:22–23), one should avoid reading 2 Corinthians in the light of Galatians, where the opponents were Judaizers.[26] Furthermore, since (in 2 Corinthians) Paul does not refute his opponents for adherence to Mosaic law at the expense of the gospel, they are most likely not Judaizers.[27]

Although they were not as severe as the Judaizers in Galatians, Paul's opponents did closely connect righteousness with the law

(11:13–15, 3:6–18).[28] Also, one should hold loosely to the idea of first-century Judaism being an extremely closed-minded system. New research exists that debunks the idea of an exclusively Pharisaic first-century Judaism.[29]

Regarding the classification of Gnostic, "it is important to recall that in the NT period the climate of thought which was eventually known as 'Gnosticism' was unsystematized."[30] Therefore, Gnosticism is "more accurately described in the first century A.D. as the espousal of 'gnostic tendencies.' "[31]

Although many of the details remain sketchy, 2 Corinthians does provide some concrete facts regarding opponents. For example, throughout the epistle Paul referred to them as "many" or a group (2:17, 10:12, 11:18). Also, the false apostles certainly came from outside Corinth (11:4–5). They did not come to town empty-handed. Instead, they arrived in Corinth with copious letters of recommendation (3:1), possibly from the church in Jerusalem. While the church in Corinth read their letters of recommendation, Paul discerned their *modus operandi*. These ungodly antagonists attempted to transpose worldly standards of success onto the office of an apostle (11:18). According to their value system, a true apostle should speak eloquently (10:10, 11:6), rule like a dictator (11:21), and command monetary support (11:7–12). In short, a true apostle stands confident in his ability. In fact, these imposters took upon themselves the title "apostle," and loved to commend themselves (2:10).

It is no accident that Paul used the word καυχάομαι (*kauchaomai*) and its cognates at least 26 times in 2 Corinthians. They ssought to portray Paul as inferior (11:5, 12:11) and themselves superior. Paul was held up to the light of their standards and judged to be inadequate. Unlike his elite opponents, Paul was far from golden-mouthed, sometimes worked a secular job, did not rule with an iron fist, and his demeanor appeared weak (10:1–2).

These standards for success played well in first-century Corinth. The fact that Paul practiced a trade and did not accept patronage certainly worked against him in Corinth.[32] In Corinth, the glory of being a self-made man ruled the day.[32] The ideology of despising the weak and praising the strong was so firmly entrenched in Corinthian society that it inevitably found its way into the church.[34] Paul wasted no time in turning these worldly, fleshly or κατά σάρκα (kata sarx) standards on their heads. For Paul, the new age (τού πνεύματος/ pneuma) had come and with it a spiritual standard for judging ministers. His perspective on true apostleship pointed away from human strength and self-reliance toward reliance on the divine. God alone makes a true apostle sufficient for the task. Paul unashamedly portrayed himself as a frail vessel, completely dependent on God (3:5, 4:7). According to Paul; the model for ministry should be Christ, not first-century Corinth. He asserted that the true minister of Christ models the suffering and resurrection of Christ (4:8–12). In other words, "the Crucified Messiah gives 'cruciform shape' to a ministry that is offered in his name."[35] Paul explained that his sufferings serve das a kind of living object lesson to the grace of God.

In other words, Paul did more than simply wear the badge of "apostle"; he lived out the true faith. When Paul sets out to defend himself he catalogues his sufferings (11:22–33). The opponents presented themselves as spiritual stars. Paul, on the other hand, pointed to his scars. In light of his standards, these imposters were merely masquerading as apostles (11:13). Paul went so far as to call them agents of Satan (11:3, 14). Their worldly measuring stick must be broken in half and thrown out of the Corinthian church.

The wonderful theology of 2 Corinthians is Paul's answer to the terrible mess in Corinth. Two prominent themes emerge in 2 Corinthians: (1) The eschatological centrality and superiority of Christ and (2) Proper new covenant ministry. In short, Paul presents Christ and the new covenant as the fulfillment of the old, answer for the present, and hope for a greater future.

1:1–1:24 Consistent Comfort in an Uncertain World

1:1–7

1. From Paul, an apostle of Jesus Christ in accordance with the will of God, and from our brother Timothy. I am writing to both the church belonging to God at Corinth and to all the saints living in the region of Achaia.

Paul's opening words, although seemingly perfunctory, serve as the seedbed for the whole letter. The Spirit ingeniously sets this verse in place like an overture in a musical score. From this launching pad, the epistle displays the development of details already infused in the first verse.

The "super apostles" have launched a vicious and relentless assault regarding Paul's ministerial credibility. They have carried the idea of their own superiority to a degree bordering on ridicule. If these false apostles can plant a rejection of Paul's authority in the hearts of the saints, they can negate his influence in the church he planted.

Thus, from a pure motive, Paul addresses himself as "an apostle of Jesus Christ in accordance with the will of God." His authority is not self-declared. Paul understands that, concerning ministry gifts, "no one takes the honor to himself, but receives it when he is called by God" (Heb. 5:4 NASB).

The phrase "in accordance with the will of God" means God intensely desired to make Paul an apostle. No matter how intensely his enemies seek to pull him down, Jesus declares him an apostle (ἀπόστολος/apostolos), meaning "one sent from a superior with authority to carry out that superior's agenda."

Paul also mentions the name of his young ministry protégé, Timothy. He seizes the opportunity to build up Timothy's reputation whenever possible. This reveals both Paul's humility regarding himself — he need not always remain in the spotlight — and his active mentoring of Timothy.

A genitive noun construction for God, τοῦ θεοῦ (*theos*), shows ownership and means "the church belonging to God" or "the church in God's possession." Believers, self-serving ministers, and certainly the devil need to be reminded that the church and all of its assets remain the property of God. Neither Paul nor any other person has ever possessed the correct currency for purchasing the church. Only the peerless blood of Jesus could secure such an infinitely valuable transaction (1 Peter 1:18–19).

The saints, which are in all Achaia, have managed to find inclusion in Paul's targeted message. Like Corinth, Achaia stood on the southern peninsula of Greece, often called the Peloponnese. The believers in this region had massive exposure to the happenings within the church at Corinth. They had, no doubt, heard the teachings of Paul's opponents. Therefore, he addresses them directly.

2. Grace and peace to you from God our Father and the Lord Jesus Christ. 3. Praise to the God and Father of our Lord Jesus Christ, the Father of all compassion and God of all comfort.

Paul's greeting of "grace and peace" from God, identical to the salutation used in 1 Corinthians, comes from the Greek translated "grace and peace" and serves as a New Testament equivalent to the Hebrew greeting *shalom*. The phrase carries the meaning of "I want you to be blessed with all the best God has to give."

4. The one comforting us in all our tribulation in order to enable us to comfort those enduring any manner of tribulation through means of the comfort with which God continually comforts us.

For "comfort," Paul employs the Greek word παρακαλέω (*parakaleo*) four times in this single sentence. The term results from an alloying of preposition παρα (*para*), meaning "near or directly beside" and the verb καλέω (*kaleo*), meaning "to call, invite, summon, or appeal to for help." The idea of one more powerful in a situation is inescapably implied. Taken together it describes one with superior power who will, when called upon to help, get closely involved in aiding the one in trouble. Jesus used this term when referring to the Holy Spirit helping believers (John 15:26).

Those in the NT need not call upon the Holy Spirit to come down and help; He remains resident within the innermost being of the believers (John 14:17). He cannot possibly get any closer than His current residence. Jesus has already called Him to live within hearts.

Paul explains that the Lord comforts us in all our tribulation. "In" springs from the most common Greek preposition in the New Testament, ἐν (en). This word manifests a good deal of flexibility. Here, the term signifies "during the time frame of." The pairing of this word with the term "all our tribulation" reveals that one simply cannot encounter a season of trouble wherein the comforter is not ready to help.

What causes the anxiety now blanketing humanity with an ever wearying heaviness? It is not the mere presence of trouble. Instead, it is the belief that in trouble, we must face things either totally alone or, at best, with those ultimately powerless to change things. Although believers do not live cocooned from trouble, they have living on the inside of themselves, "a very present help in trouble" (Ps. 46:1). When believers find themselves in trouble, they only need realize that the remedy for trouble lives in them and they are in Him.

5. For just as the sufferings of Christ abound in us, comfort also abounds in us through Christ.

The "sufferings of Christ" refers to believers laying down their own agendas, comfort, and very selves while advancing God's kingdom on earth. Paul's mention of these sufferings in no way points to things such as sickness or poverty. The Father has no desire to put on His sons and daughters what His only begotten Son has already both taken on Himself and taken away. Instead, πάθημα (pathema) speaks of hardship associated with the laying down of self to the point of, if necessary in spreading the good news, death. Such sacrifice makes way for real resurrection power. No wonder Paul prays out earnestly, "that I may know Him and the power of His resurrection, and the fellowship of His sufferings ($\pi \acute{\alpha} \theta \eta \mu \alpha$)" (Phil 3:10 NKJ).

> **6. If we experience affliction, it is for your comfort and salvation, which is workable for enduring the same afflictions which we endure. If we experience comfort, it is for your comfort and salvation. 7. Thus our hope for you remains strong, because we know that just as you share in afflictions, you will also surely share in comfort.**

In verse 6, Paul contends that he serves as a living example of suffering hardship in order to bless others. He boldly states, "Although we may now be afflicted with trouble, once we, with the help of the Comforter, come through this, we will comfort you."

1:8–14

> **8. Brothers, we did not want you to remain unaware concerning the trouble we experienced in Asia. We were pressed down by heavy trouble to a level beyond anything our own strength could support, so that the circumstances offered no hope of survival.**

The great trials Paul encountered in Asia, while not sent by God, drove him to God. When difficulty assails greatly, victorious believers wholeheartedly refuse to fold. They make a choice to not recoil from the Word, prayer, and church. When the waves of affliction crash against the ship, tear the sails, and fill the boat, they refuse to cower. Instead, they jump into a water-walking lesson with the Son of God.

When believers find themselves saying, "I cannot take it for another second," the Lord says, "I can and therefore, you will. For it's not by your own strength or ability, but by my Spirit" (Zech. 4:6). Paul believes that God will fulfill His promises no matter what things looked like outwardly. Circumstances offer no hope whatsoever;

ἐξαπορέομαι (exaporeo) means despairing of all hope. In fact, they scream with ferocity, "The end has come!"

Here, Paul does not proclaim, like some translations seem to say, "I have lost hope." Instead, he contends that, while hope in the natural has vanished, his hope in God remains steadfast. No matter what happens, God's promise will not fall to the ground.

Like Paul, Abraham faced a dilemma where circumstances aligned to signal no hope of the fulfillment of God's promise. The man God called "the father of the nations" had not a single offspring via his wife. Furthermore, his wife had aged far past her years of fertility. Nevertheless, "Even when there was no reason for hope, Abraham kept hoping — believing that he would become the father of many nations. For God had said to him, "That's how many descendants you will have!" (Rom. 4:18 NLT). As a result, "Abraham's faith did not weaken, even though, at about 100 years of age, he figured his body was as good as dead — and so was Sarah's womb" (Rom. 4:19 NLT).

Even the prospect of death itself cannot move one standing in faith on God's promises. When told to offer up his only son, "Abraham reasoned that if Isaac died, God was able to bring him back to life again. And in a sense, Abraham did receive his son back from the dead." (Heb. 11:19 NLT).

9. In fact, we had in ourselves the sentence of death. This allowed us to not trust in ourselves, but in God who raises the dead. 10. He rescued us from massive danger, and he will certainly rescue us again. For we have placed our hope in him and he will rescue us again. 11. You are helping us by praying for us. This will result in many people expressing thanks to God for showing favor on our behalf.

Similarly, as the devil turned up the heat on Paul, even to the point of death, he trusted in God who raises the dead.

12. This is what we boast about: the testimony of our clear conscience. We conducted ourselves with sincerity and godly motives and not with fleshly wisdom, but in the grace of God.

**We behaved this way in our dealings with the world and espe-
cially toward you. 13. For we have only written what you both
read and can clearly understand [there is no hidden message
in it]. Now, I hope that you will understand this to the end
14. even if you don't currently understand it all. Then, on the
day the Lord Jesus comes, you will boast about us just as we
currently do about you.**

In verse 12, Paul begins to once again argue sternly for his own
credibility. In addition to holding a clear conscience, Paul has conducted himself rightly in both the world and, especially, in his dealings with the Corinthians. This does not mean Paul behaved better in the presence of the Corinthian church than in general society.
However, his regular interaction with the church afforded it far more
opportunities to watch him closely. This is Paul's way of saying, "You
watched me very closely while I spent time there. I have no shame
about how I lived out the faith."

1:15–24

**15. In this confidence I purposed to come to you before, so
that you might have two opportunities for blessing: 16. One
on my way to Macedonia and again on my return trip from
Macedonia. Then you could send me on to Judea. 17. Was I
vacillating when I made this plan? Or do I make plans according to fleshly motives so that I can say "yes, yes" when I
am intending "no, no"? 18. In accordance with God's faithfulness, our word to you did not fluctuate between "yes"
and "no." 19. For the Jesus Christ, the Son of God, who was
preached to you by us (me, Silas, and Timothy) was not "yes"
and then "no," but in him it was and will forever be "yes."**

While defending his character in verse 15, Paul explains why, after
saying he would return soon, he has yet to visit. Paul planned on
coming through Corinth twice; however, circumstances beyond his
control made the trip undoable. This provides fuel for his opponents
to accuse him of not keeping his word.

Insecure people search out and happily capitalize on opportunities for discrediting the reputation of others. Immature believers often give ear to such poisonous talk falling from the mouth of the insecure. Without question, a stubborn carnality in Corinth provided a massive and abundantly fertile seedbed for the planting of gossip (1Cor. 3:1–4).

20. For no matter how great in number and scope God's promises, they are all "yes" in Him. And we speak the "amen" (let it be shown true) to God. 21. Now He who establishes us, along with you, in Christ is God. He anointed us,

The Lord always says exactly what He means and means what He says. The word "all" in verse 20 comes from the Greek term ὅσος (ho-sos), meaning "as great as," "as far as," "as many as," and "as much as." Therefore, no matter how many or how great the promises of God, they are all yes in Him. When standing side by side, Satan's attacks appear not nearly "as great as" the infinitely greater promises of God. No promise the Lord has made finds fulfillment when circumstances align favorably. Its accomplishment has zero dependency on circumstances. God's promises, like believers, find their working out in Him. Furthermore, when God manifests the fulfillment of a promise, it brings Him glory through us. God gains no joy from observing His children under the weight of sickness, lack, or any kind of defeat. However, it brings Him great glory when the Word finds fulfillment in His own body!

22. stamped us with his mark of exclusive ownership, and gave us the first payment guaranteeing the balloon payment promised us.

The *New King James Version* translates Paul's description of the Spirit here as both a "seal" and a "down payment." The word translated "seal" comes from the Greek term σφραγίζω (sphragizo) meaning "to set a mark of authentication or ownership upon a person or thing." Greek writers employed the term to describe a king's stamping of his signet ring into either wet clay or hot wax. Upon either material hardening, the sovereign's mark of authenticity remained for all to see. Those purchased with blood from the King's Son, have placed upon them a "mark" signifying God's authentic property.

This imagery shows up big in Revelation when an angel places a protective "mark" (σφραγίς/sphragis) upon those protected from the plagues of wrath (Rev. 9:4). Conversely, John employs a different word conveying the same concept when speaking of the "mark (χάραγμα/charagma) of the beast." Like σφραγίς, χάραγμα speaks of an irreversible exchange. Those receiving the χάραγμα accept the Antichrist's provision and protection in exchange for his ownership of their very personhood.

Amazingly, the Spirit not only marks believers as God's authentic property, He also gives them a down payment on the fullness of redemption. The word translated "earnest" (KJV) comes from the Greek term ἀρραβών (arrhabon). This word concerns the "first payment of an extensive financial contract." One only need to produce a ἀρραβών for larger scale contracts. The Lord has an incalculably large contract to bless his children! ἀρραβών describes the funds guaranteeing the fulfillment of the remaining portion of the contract with all its benefits.

The greatness of the Spirit on earth trumps anything the devil can possibly set forth. However, a balloon payment waits in the bank of heaven bearing the name of every faithful believer. While the down payment proves far more than enough, what awaits dwarfs it. Peter encourages believers to remember that they possess, "an inheritance incorruptible and undefiled and that does not fade away, reserved in heaven for you" (1Peter 1:4 NKJ). In the end, "He who overcomes shall inherit all things" (Rev. 21:7 NKJ). While man may back out of contracts, the Lord always keeps His Word. "He is not a man, so he does not lie. He is not human, so he does not change his mind" (Num. 23:19 NLT).

23. Furthermore, I call God as a witness concerning my truthfulness of my intentions. I did not return to Corinth in order to spare you another confrontation.

**24. Not that we lead through dominating your faith with in-
timidation. Instead, we are workers together for your joy; for
by your own faith you stand.**

While defending his character, Paul goes so far as to say, "Now I
call upon God as my witness that I am telling the truth. The reason I
didn't return to Corinth was to spare you from a severe rebuke" (NLT).
With confidence, he states, "I call upon God to testify regarding the
purity of my intentions." The word often translated "witness" or "testify" comes from the Greek term μάρτυς (*martus*) meaning "a legal
witness" or "a witness testifying to the veracity of an event." A witness
can boldly say, "I saw firsthand what occurred."

The term translated "soul" comes from the Greek word ψυχή
(*psuche*), meaning "the seat of one's mind, emotions, and intentions."
Here, Paul contends, "I call God, as a firsthand witness, regarding my
intentions to visit you." He assures them a genuine love, not confusing
communication, proves the motivating factor in his lack of visitation.

2:1–17 The Fragrance of Forgiveness

2:1–9

1. So I decided that I would not make another painful visit. 2. For if I cause you sorrow, who could then make me joyful? Certainly not the one I just made sorrowful. 3. That's exactly why I wrote what I did, so that when I arrive, I won't be made sorrowful by the people who ought to disburse joy. You must know that I derive great happiness from knowing you are filled with joy. 4. I wrote to you from a heart squeezed on all sides with concern and affliction. As the words flowed onto the page, so did my tears. My goal was not to fill you with sorrow, but I sought to make you aware of my overflowing love for you.

Paul continues to explain why he hadn't visited Corinth as previously planned. Paul sought to spare them another sorrowful visit. He had to clean up several messes during his previous visit. Additionally, Paul had to confront, via the letter of 1 Corinthians, the church's failure to deal with open sin in the lives of its members. He needed time both to pray and allow them to act on his earlier letter. These verses reveal Paul's heart of immense compassion for the Corinthians. Although necessary, he administered church discipline with sorrow of heart, tears, and fatherly love.

5. I am not speaking over the top by telling you that the one who caused you sorrow hurt you much more than he did me.

Here, he addresses the matter of the church member living in an incestuous relationship. Paul tells the church, "the one who caused you sorrow hurt you much more than he did me." In other words, Paul knows that although he had responsibility *to* those in the church, he cannot take responsibility *for* one's poor decisions. He certainly hurt for this man caught in the trap of sin, even though he willingly jumped into the cage. However, watching rot spread through the tissue of the church via a "little leaven" caused him much more sorrow. He hurt knowing that such actions, especially if not corrected, fostered infection in the body.

6. The punishment doled out by the most of you proved sufficient.

Paul commends them for following his instructions in 1 Corinthians to "throw this man out and hand him over to Satan" (1 Cor. 5:5 NLT). While this may sound exceptionally harsh, it, like all proper church discipline, carried redemptive intentions. The desired outcome was, "so that his sinful nature will be destroyed and he himself will be saved on the day the Lord returns."

7. Now, the time has come to forgive and comfort him. If not, he might drown by drinking down regret.

Thankfully, Paul's plan of discipline and restoration worked much faster than expected. The incestuous man showed genuine repentance and sought to reconnect with the church. At this point, the church had driven the train of church discipline a bit too far down the tracks; they adamantly refused to readmit the repentant man. Here, Paul exhorts the Corinthians to "forgive and comfort him."

The word translated "forgive" comes from the Greek term χαρίζομαι (*charizomai*). This word excels above the much more common word for forgive. In addition to meaning "to cancel out a debt," χαρίζομαι also connotes "doing something kind for a person." It involves going beyond wiping a slate clean to actually transferring something good. God does this same thing for those exercising faith in Him. The Lord takes away everything negative in the believer's spiritual account. However, He never stops there. God then transfers all of His righteousness into the freshly balanced account of the believer. Thus, one's account moves from an impossibly negative amount to a zero balance and then into the very abundance of heaven.

The word translated "comfort" is a form of παρακαλέω, the same word detailed in 2 Corinthians 1:4. This level of help welcomes the repentant believer back into the church. Furthermore, it lets him know, "we are here to help, not castigate." If not, he may be "swallowed up with sorrow" and the restoration process foiled.

The Greek term καταπίνω (katapino) used in the last part of verse 7 is a compound word from the prefix κατα (kata) meaning "down," and πίνω (pino) meaning "drink." Thus, the word means, "to swallow alive" or "drown." Here, the subjunctive, passive verb construction conveys the thought, "he has the very real possibility of drowning in condemnation." When the church throws out the lifesaver of forgiveness and comfort, it keeps the repentant person afloat in the truth.

8. Therefore, I am urging you to validate your love to him. 9. I also wrote to test you regarding your compliance with my instructions.

In verse 8, Paul urges them to validate their "love to him." This reaffirms God's never-ending love to the one assailed by waves of condemnation. At the point of temptation, the enemy says, "Go ahead and do it. It's really no big deal." However, after yielding to temptation; the conviction of the Holy Spirit seizes the offender, brings the light of truth regarding the ugliness of sin, and extends the gift of repentance. At that moment, Satan speaks the lie, "You are a terrible example of a Christian. How could God possibly forgive you? People will judge you harshly for this for years." Against the darkness of these death-dealing lies, the church must hold forth the life-giving light of truth.

On the front end, believers must hold one another accountable to live godly in Christ Jesus. No matter how gracefully one attempts to dance around God's Word with clever theological costumes, the Bible states, "The one who sins will die" (Ezek. 18:20). The lie to the contrary first entered this world from the lips of the Serpent in the garden in the form of "You will not actually die [if you sin]" (Gen. 3:4). Since that time, it has reappeared countless times in ever changing packaging.

On the back end, when one seeks to escape the stranglehold of disobedience via repentance, the church must extend the same hand Jesus did to the woman caught in adultery. Restoration, not condemnation flows from the throne to every person seeking forgiveness. Ironically, those choosing to shun the repentant by operating with punitive rather than restorative motives have unwittingly wrapped themselves in sinful behavior.

2:10–14

10. When you forgive a person, I also forgive. Whatever I forgave, I did so in the person of Christ

Paul then notes that he forgives the person as well. He does so in the person of Christ. This phrase means two things. First, Paul offers forgiveness freely in Christ's presence because Christ forgave him. How could Paul justly look into the face of the one who forgave him while refusing to dispense forgiveness to others? He exposes this same truth to the church at Colossae by saying, "Forgive anyone who offends you. Remember, the Lord forgave you, so you must forgive others" (Col. 3:13 NLT).

In addition, the phrase speaks of the apostolic authority Christ has given to Paul. He exercised that same authority when handing down the judgment of "turning the man over to Satan." This decision sprang, not from a personal vindictiveness, but from Paul's deep desire to help the entire church.

Now, he asserts: "I forgive whatever needs to be forgiven; I do so with Christ's authority for your benefit (2 Cor. 2:10 NLT). Just as permitting open sin would hurt the church, at this juncture, harboring unforgiveness would certainly result in harm. Therefore, Paul forgives for the benefit of both the individual and the whole.

11. in order that Satan will not gain an advantage over us. For we are not clueless to recognize his crafty plans.

This phrase, "gain an advantage" come from the Greek term πλεονεκτέω (pleonekteo) meaning "to take more ground from another than one has a right to." Believers should give no real estate to the devil (Eph. 4:27) via unforgiveness. Instead, they should not be ignorant of such satanic devices.

Here, Paul places ρλεονεκτέω in its subjunctive passive form πλεονεκτηθῶμεν. Writers use the subjunctive verb mood to convey a strong possibility of something taking place without reaching inevitable certainty. This verse leads off with the Greek term ἵνα meaning "so that" or "in order that." In this case, ἵνα links directly to Paul's discussion of forgiveness in the preceding verse. The phrase "crafty plans" comes from the Greek word νόημα (noema) often meaning "design of the mind." Thus, Paul warns the church, "Holding tightly to unfogiveness positions you for the strong possibility of Satan gaining territory in your minds." Once firmly planted, the tree of unforgivenss sprouts forth the immensely bitter fruits of revenge and paranoia within one's thought life. These thoughts come out of one's mouth in the form of "They will one day get what's coming to them" and "They are always looking for ways to hurt me." Conversely, forgiveness thwarts the possibility for demonic weeds and affords the free flow of Divine life.

The word "clueless" comes from the Greek verb ἀγνοέω (agnoeo). This word forms from the word γινώσκω meaning "to have knowledge of something" and the prefix ἀ signifying "without" or "totally lacking." Thus ἀγνοέω means "to be totally without knowledge of a thing, person, or event." In modern, colloquial speech, one would say "clueless."

Here, Paul places the term in the present tense to signify continuous action meaning, "we are never in a state of not knowing Satan's devices." ἀγνοέω can also mean "disregard." Although believers ought not focus the lion's share of their attention on the enemy's plans, they dare not disregard them.

Some teach that in the new covenant dispensation, no attention should go to the enemy. This line of reasoning states that, "the battle is already over, and we don't ever need to fight." Somehow Paul, the author of several New Covenant books, failed to get that message. Peter agrees with Paul by saying, "Stay alert! Watch out for your great enemy, the devil. He prowls around like a roaring lion, looking for someone to devour" (1 Peter 5:8 NLT).

Interestingly, the word translated "prowls around" sits in the present tense. This means that the enemy never stops looking for an opportunity to pounce. Also, for the word translated "devour," Peter uses the exact same word (καταπίνω) he employs in verse 7 discussed earlier.

The word translated "plans" springs from the Greek term meaning "mind," "design," or "purpose." This speaks of a well-thought-out plan purposed on deceiving believers. Satan seeks to implant thoughts into the minds of believers. Paul asserts that unforgiveness both fosters new and fuels already constructed strongholds in the mind (2 Cor. 10:4–5).

12. When I came to Troas to preach the Gospel of Christ, the Lord opened for me a door of great opportunity.

Earlier in the epistle, Paul explained how his failure to visit Corinth resulted not from dishonest communication but circumstances beyond control (2 Cor. 1:15–24). Now he brings them up to speed regarding his activities since his last appearance.

Paul had travelled from Ephesus to Troas for the purpose of preaching. There he found the Lord opened a door for a very successful evangelistic campaign. Paul often uses the phrase, "the Lord opened for me a door" to describe grand opportunities to reach the lost (cf. 1 Cor. 16:9, Col. 4:3). In Revelation, Jesus states that He opens doors no person can possibly shut (Rev. 3:8).

13. Nevertheless, I could never relax because my brother Titus had not arrived. So I said goodbye to them and left for Macedonia.

Although he held this amazing possibility, Paul left prematurely due to his love for the Corinthians. While in Troas, Paul planned on seeing Titus (who had delivered the "severe letter" to Corinth) for the purpose of being briefed about the Corinthian response to that letter.

When Titus failed to show, Paul became restless. He had no rest in his spirit.

The word translated "rest" comes from the Greek term ἄνεσις meaning "rest," "relaxation," or "loosening up." Paul said, "I could not ever relax" until I saw Titus. Paul begins taking the road to Macedonia in hopes of crossing paths with Titus, but after arriving, Paul still had yet to find him. Therefore, "when we arrived in Macedonia, there was no rest for us. We faced conflict from every direction" (2 Cor. 7:5 NLT).

14. Now thank God who is always leading us to triumph in Christ! Through this he is making obvious the fragrance of his knowledge in everywhere.

Upon a surface reading, verse 14 appears arbitrarily dropped into the chapter. However, the reason for Paul's outburst of joy reveals itself in 2 Corinthians 7 — he found Titus! Not only did the two reunite, but Titus gave Paul a good report regarding the Corinthian church's response to his severe letter (2 Cor. 7:6–9).

Even though believers endure times of hardship, before long, God always leads them "to triumph in Christ." This phrase comes from the Greek word θριαμβεύω (thriambeuo). Greek writers assigned this term to Roman military victory parades. These "triumphs" showed forth the greatness of the particular field general. The general marched before a mass of dignitaries along with his vice leaders, treasures taken from the enemy, and defeated nobles in chains. The procession ended at a temple to Jupiter wherein the general offered fragrant incense to the false god.

When victory manifests in the lives of believers, the Lord gets glory by showing forth the fragrance of His knowledge in every place.

2:15–17

15. For our lives send up to God the pleasing fragrance of Christ. This fragrance is processed differently by those being saved and those who are headed toward eternal lostness.

16. To the one we give off a fragrance of death signifying their own impending death. To the other, we dispense a life giving fragrance. Who is suitable for a task this important?

Under the old covenant priestly system, animal sacrifices caused a pleasing odor to come before God. Under the new covenant, the great High Priest "loved us and gave himself up for us as a fragrant offering and sacrifice to God" (Eph. 5:2 NIV). Now the believer's obedience in the face of trial disburses an odor in the spirit realm. Like Paul, Noah serves as a living example of this truth. He first "did everything as the Lord commanded him. (Gen. 7:5 NLT). Then, his obedience endured a time of trial while in the ark.

Afterward, when he offered the sacrifices, "the Lord smelled the pleasing aroma" (Gen. 8:21 NIV). In the Septuagint, "aroma" is the same Greek word (εὐωδία/euodia) used here by Paul. The scent of obedience infuses the entire atmosphere with the message that Jesus is Lord. This occurs in every place (life circumstance). In fact, the tougher the place, the more pleasing the aroma.

Sadly, not everyone loves the aroma of obedience. The phrase "are being saved" comes from the present tense Greek participle σῳζομένοις (sozo). This verb construction conveys an ongoing process. Of course, redeemed believers find this aroma pleasing. However, so do those in the process of being saved: those not actively hardening their hearts to the Lord. Conversely, those in the process of purposely moving away from God find the scent repugnant. It brings to their attention their own undeniable unrighteousness.

The writer of Proverbs picks up this theme when he proclaims, "An unjust man *is* an abomination to the righteous, And *he who* is upright in the way *is* an abomination to the wicked" (Prov. 29:27 NKJ). Here, the word translated as "abomination" comes from the Hebrew word תּוֹעֵבָה (towebah) meaning "a thing giving off an intesenly foul odor."

The apostle John reminds believers that the world will, at times, hate them for walking in obedience. He notes that Cain killed Abel "because his own actions were evil and his brothers were righteous" (1 John 3:12 NIV). In similar fashion, when Stephen spoke, the stone hearted crowd aggressively "covered their ears" (Acts 7:57). When believers walk in sacrificial obedience, the world often covers their noses.

17. For we are not like many who peddle God's word like mere merchandise. Instead, we speak sincerely as those sent from God in Christ.

Paul caps off this section with another appeal to his integrity. The *New International Version* says "Unlike so many, we do not peddle the word of God for profit." The word translated "peddle" comes from the Greek term καπηλεύω (*kapeleuo*) meaning "to trade something for personal profit." Paul argues that many unashamedly use the gospel as a means for funding personal agendas. Deceitful ministers cloaking a hunger for personal gain in the garb of real giftings may fool some people. Nevertheless, God's eyes work well.

3:1–18 The Weighty Glory of the New Covenant

3:1–5

1. Do we need to begin to praise ourselves again? Do we really need to either bring letters of recommendation to you or receive them from you?

Paul throws a sarcastic jab at his opponents who relentlessly present themselves as having it all together. These itinerate speakers travel weighted down with the recommendations of others. They drop names like storm clouds dispense rain. Of course, while in Corinth they have already begun working on securing a recommendation from the Corinthians. Paul chooses to present Christ rather than himself. He seeks, above all, the recommendation of God shown forth in the power of the Spirit to minister.

2. You yourselves serve as our letter, written in our hearts, known and read by everyone.

In securing endorsements for his ministry, Paul has no interest in either the nods of prominent socialites or the written affirmations of fame seekers. Transformed lives hang as fruit on the tree of Paul's ministry.

3. The results of our ministry are being manifestly declared by the letter of your life. This letter has been written, not with the stroke of an inked pen, but with the Spirit of the living God. It is carved, not on tablets hewn out of stone, but on the writing surface [hard drive] of your hearts. 4. We have such great confidence through Christ toward God.

Paul invested in the Corinthians to the point where they became written on the hard drive of his heart. Because Paul's heart is an open book, anyone can "recognize and read the results" of his ministry.

The proof of Paul's ministry does not rest upon the foundation of mere words. Rather than words on a page, the Corinthians manifestly declare the truth poured from God, through Paul, and into their hearts. Since the fall, men have emptied an ocean of ink onto a nearly innumerable number of writing surfaces to create a mountain of recommendations. However, only the Holy Spirit can write love on the human heart.

5. Our qualifications do not spring from ourselves. We do not consider ourselves self-sufficient, but our adequacy comes from being in God.

Paul rounds out this section of Scripture by stating that, in himself, he has nothing substantive to offer. This does not display a false humility deceptively clothed in self-deprecation. Paul has confidence in his calling. Nevertheless, he acknowledges that all he has of value came from God. Any success Paul enjoys in ministry springs from his cooperation with God's grace. He sums up this truth by asserting, "Whatever I am now, it is all because God poured out his special favor on me — and not without results. For I have worked harder than any of the other apostles; yet it was not I but God who was working through me by his grace" (1 Cor. 15:10 NLT).

3:6–11

Verses 6 through 11 of chapter 3 require a more thorough treatment than any other portion of 2 Corinthians. Great confusion regarding the interrelation of the Old and New Testaments necessitates such an extended exposition. The devil knows that a proper understanding of this issue will launch the church into a drastically higher level of maturity. The detailing of these verses includes many outside sources. This blesses readers with a survey of what other scholars say on the matter.

Those unfamiliar with Greek grammar may find parts of this section a bit heavy at times. However, any grammatical discussions relate directly to the real-life issues at hand. Prepare yourself to step into the deep end of God's revelatory pool.

Before investigating verse 6, a brief word about the interaction of the two testaments is in order. "Just how do the old and new covenants relate to each other?" In one form or another this question has graced the ears of pastors and scholars across the continuum of church history. From Paul to the present, humanity has pondered how to handle these two sublime covenants. Efforts to respond have produced damaging extremes on both ends of the spectrum.[1]

On one end stand those who view the old and new covenants as inherently one. Thus, there exists no truly "new" covenant. Instead, the so-called new covenant is really a fresh expression of the one and only covenant made with Israel. Many Christians holding to this position display a strange longing to become Jewish.

Without question, the New Testament rests upon the foundation of the Old. Israel served as the vehicle which brought the Messiah to all, including the church. For this reason, the study of the Old Testament forever remains of massive value. However, sometimes well-meaning efforts to "return to our Jewish roots" veils a clear view of the "better covenant established on more advantageous promises" (Heb. 8:6). Talk of God really moving now that we have blown the shofar, donned a prayer shawl, and made the trek to Israel — in themselves such practices can provide a great deal of blessing — can manifest a misguided sense of direction. This perspective leads to the drawing of lines between "regular" (Gentile) Christians and "really spiritual" (Messianic Jewish) Christians.[2]

On the opposite pole stand those who vehemently contend for complete discontinuity between the covenants. Too often, in the spirit of Marcion, the old covenant is degraded almost to the point of uselessness. Preachers in this stream of belief have a good deal of doctrinal confusion in their water. They forget that the New Testament refers to the Old Testament — all of it — as "the Word of God" (2 Tim. 3:16). A great error exists in shirking personal moral responsibility by brushing aside thirty-nine books of Scripture with the cavalier phrase, "that's Old Testament."

Over the last ten years, a new fervor to further besmirch the Old Testament has arisen. Preachers go so far as to downplay the words of Jesus because, "that was before the new covenant went into force." Thankfully, divine providence strategically prepared and positioned a unique individual to address this issue. Paul's intense training in the old covenant, coupled with personal revelations from Jesus certainly qualify him to tackle this issue. It is indeed remarkable that one so well versed and immersed in the law became the "apostle to the Gentiles." In addition, the Pauline literary corpus provides a mountain of material on the interrelation of the covenants. More specifically, in 2 Corinthians 3:6–11, Paul argues that God has indeed set up a new covenant. Furthermore, although the old covenant was glorious, it was temporary and anticipated the new — modern day Judaizers cover your ears — superior and abiding covenant.

6. He has qualified us as ministers of the New Covenant, not by means of the letter (of the law), but of the Spirit. For the letter (written code) kills, but the Spirit gives life.

Paul asserts the miracle that the maker, sustainer, redeemer, and judge of the universe "qualified" him as an able minister of the new covenant. The term translated "covenant" comes from the Greek compound word διαθήκης (diatheke) comprised of θήκη (theke, a container, box, or chest) alloyed with the prefixed preposition διά (dia). In the genitive construction, διά is used to signify instrumentation (the means by which a thing occurs). Thus, διαθήκης (covenant) expresses a container serving as the means by which God communicates His will. Into this container, He pours himself!

Under the old covenant, the "ark of the covenant" served as this receptacle. However, under the new covenant, the believer is the container. In the Old, God's visible glory shone bright above the ark. Under the new, the glory rests both within and flows out from the heart of believers.

The Lord has woven this truth, in seamless perfection, throughout this chapter. The carriers of God's presence have a responsibility to let this glory shine in sacrificial love, holy living, and signs and wonders. Believers must embody both the character and authority of the covenant residing within them; "The letter kills, but the Spirit makes alive."

Over the years this portion of verse 6 has "been subject to all sorts of hermeneutical gerrymandering."[3] In the early centuries of Christianity, many used this phrase to imply a spiritual versus literal reading of the text. In more recent times, these words have been misused to degrade any academic study of Scripture. Admittedly, taken by itself, this portion of verse 6 leaves much for the imagination. Paul's language must be taken in context of his other epistles. Indeed, "a sentence so pregnant as this, and so capable of various applications, must have been very perplexing to the Corinthians, had they not been fairly acquainted beforehand with the Apostles' form of doctrine."[4]

The immediate literary context shows that γράμμα (gramma, written code) refers, not to the entire Old Testament canon, but to the Mosaic covenant. It should be noted that Paul never seeks to degrade the law itself. In fact, he views the law as "holy," "just," "good," and "spiritual" (Rom. 7:12, 14). Instead, Paul attacks the use of the law as a means to righteousness (Rom. 3:20, 10:1–4; Phil. 3:2–9).[5] In spite of strong rabbinic support to the contrary,[6] the law cannot give life (Gal. 3:21) to sinful man. Although the law is spiritual, only the Spirit (who infuses the new covenant) can give life (ζωοποιεῖ/zoopoieo). Therefore, in the new age, any dependence on the Mosaic covenant is a serious retrogression.[7]

7. Now if the ministry of death in letters engraved on stone (engraved into stone) came with glory, so that the sons of Israel were not able to stare intently at the face of Moses because of the glory of his face, glory which was fading 8. how will not the ministry of the Spirit be with greater glory? (how much more glorious will be the ministry of the Spirit?)

The Greek of verses 7 and 8 forms a long, complex sentence. The construction contains a first-class conditional phrase. In this instance, because his audience already agrees with him concerning the protasis, Paul urges them to realize the truth of the apodasis.[8] The presence of εἰ δέ (ei de) . . . πῶς οὐχί μᾶλλον (pos ochi mallon) — if . . . then how will it not be even more — signals the beginning of Paul's midrash of Exodus 34:29 through 35. Interestingly, he calls the Mosaic law ἡ διαοκνία τόν θανάτον (diakonia thanatos) which translates "the ministry of death."

This description of the law (similar to τό γάρ γράμμα ἀποκτέννει/ gar gramma apokteino meaning "for the writing kills") in verse 6 seems to speak evil of the Mosaic covenant. However, like the phrase in verse 6, this description must be understood in light of the entire Pauline corpus. When taken in this context, the phrase διαοκνία τόν θανάτον refers to the effects of the law on sinful man (Rom. 7:10–11). Moses presented Israel with God's law and warned them that disobedience would result in death (Deut. 30:15–18).

In addition, the very form of the *qal wayyomer* (from lesser good to the greater good) argument indicates that Paul was not attempting to discredit the law.[9] The death was a result of man's failure (without the Spirit) to keep the law of God. The phrase ἐν γράμμασιν ἐντετυπωμένη λίθοις (en gramma entupoo lithos) — writing engraved in stone — refers to the Ten Commandments written on stone tablets (Ex. 34:1, 4). This phrase may also refer back to 2 Corinthians 3:1–3, where the letters of recommendation are contrasted with what was written (ἐγγεγραμμένη/eggrapho) by the Spirit on human hearts.[10] Contextually, this verse stands surrounded by a theme of ministerial credibility and the issue of proper credentials. Paul goes on to say that the ministry of death ἐγενήθη ἐν δόξή (ginomai doxa) — "came in with glory."

Although the word δοξα was used in the secular sphere to mean "opinion," "reputation," or "pride," it took on a higher level of meaning in the LXX (Septuagint) and New Testament.[11] The idea of δοξα to signify brightness was certainly a result of septuagintal influence. The LXX employs δοξα to translate the Hebrew words *hodh* (splendor) and *kabhodl* (splendor, honor). For example, Isaiah 60:1 declares that "your light has come and the *kabhodh* (δοξα) of the Lord rises upon you." Thus in the Old Testament, the δοξα of the Lord was "the immediate presence of Yahweh."[12]

In the New Testament, this same δοξα appeared on the Mount of Transfiguration (Luke 9:32), in *του θεού έν προσώπω, [Ιησου] Χριστου* (*theos en prosopon Iesous Christos*) for "face of Jesus Christ" (2 Cor. 4:6) and on the Damascus Road (Acts 9:3, 22:11). Without question, Paul's personal encounter with the glory utterly changed both his theology and praxis. The autobiographical tone (Paul's high degree of self-disclosure) and doctrinal issues of 2 Corinthians both contribute to Paul's heavy usage of δοξα.[13]

Next, Paul uses an adverbial infinitive construction that expresses result (*ὥστε μη . . . ἀτενίσαι/ hoste may atenizo*).[14] In other words, the law came with such great glory that the Israelites could not "look (stare) at the face of Moses." This glory, although intensely potent, was certainly *καταργουμένην* (katargeo), or "waning."

Although *καταργουμένην* is often translated as "fading," the term annulled or abolished demands consideration.[15] In Paul's writings, *καταργέω* (and its cognates) refer to what is invalid, annulled, or in the process of being replaced.[16] Furthermore, if Paul wished to convey the idea of fading, he could have used a word such as *ἀφανισμός* (*apanismos*), "vanishing from view," as he did in Hebrews 8:13. The use of the passive participle (*καταργουμένην/katargeo*) implies that God is the subject of the abolition, while the present tense indicates that this abolition began when the glory *ἐγενήθη* (*ginomai*), or "came on the scene."

In other words, "the apostle does not mean to say here that the brightness on Moses' face was destined to fade, but that it was fading."[18] Obviously, the Exodus narrative does not mention the fading glory of Moses's face. Indeed, "Paul goes beyond his Exodus text at a number of points."[19] As mentioned earlier, Paul begins now a midrashic type of interpretation.

Verse 8 is a type of literary hinge for Paul's argument. In light of the evidence presented in verses 6 and 7, Paul boldly asks the rhetorical question, "How much more will the ministry of the Spirit be glorious?" At this point, he reinforces what has already been said and opens the way for further comparison. For Paul, the new covenant glory has a far greater, eternal glory. This Spirit empowered, heart written covenant both comes with and produces greater glory. Under the new covenant, believers that walk in the Spirit satisfy God's requirements of δικαιοσύνη (dikaiosune, "righteousness").

9. For if the ministry of condemnation came with glory, much more the ministry of righteousness abounds in glory.

In verse 9, Paul offers another point of demarcation between the covenants. In verse 6, he contrasted the opposite concepts of life and death. Now, he contrasts the opposites righteousness and condemnation. The old stood as the "ministry of condemnation." The word translated "condemnation" comes from the Greek term κατάκρισις (katakrisis). This compound word is constructed from word κρίσις meaning "judgment" and the prefixed preposition κατά meaning "down." Therefore, κατάκρισις means "to bring down judgment." Although the word appears only here and in 7:3, it shares a close affinity to κατάκριμα (used in Rom. 5: 6, 18, 8:1).[20]

In summation, one under the law stands condemned, as a lawbreaker (Jer. 31:32, 34), to certain spiritual death. This line of reasoning runs throughout both Romans 5 through 7 and Galatians 3:19 through 22. More specifically, Romans 5:17 and 18 makes a remarkably similar contrast between "life" and "death." The only answer to this inescapable condemnation is ἡ διακονία τῆς δικαιοσύνης (diakonia dikaiosune), or "the ministry of righteousness."

The noun δικαιοσύνη (righteousness) is a favorite of Paul in 2 Corinthians.[21] Here, ἡ διακονία τῆς δικαιοσύνης carries a "forensic" meaning such as forgiveness, acquittal, or vindication.[22] As mentioned earlier, this new covenant ministry has brought the experience of righteousness through the power of the Spirit of God (1 Cor. 1:30).

Paul personally experienced the law of Moses in a powerful way, yet he was floored when greeted by the covenant of righteousness. Thus, compared to the old, the Spirit-filled ministry of righteousness "overflows with abundance" (περισσεύω/perisseuo) in glory. Paul often uses περισσεύω to describe the new age of salvation in contrast to the former age.[23] The idea of a new era fits well with "the ministry of the Spirit" detailed in verse 8. That point stands as the first time Paul presents the Spirit as an eschatological reality rending the old covenant obsolete.[24]

In Romans, Paul uses περισσεύεω and its cognates to express the magnitude of the grace of God. Where the enormous measure of sin threatened to doom humanity, God's grace did much more ὑπερεπερίσσευσεν (huperperisseuo). This compound word is comprised of περισσεύεω and the prefixed preposition ὑπερ (huper) meaning "over the top" or "super." Therefore, in light of sin's condemning force, grace provided "super, way over the top" forgiveness (Rom. 5:20). Without question, this word signifies a fullness that abounds and overflows. In "this process of overflowing, the existing standards and rules are transcended, and what was comparable becomes incomparable."[25] This acquitting righteousness acts as a solar eclipse on the lesser light of the ministry of condemnation.

10. Indeed, in this case, what was glorious was not glorious on account of the surpassing glory.

In verse 10, Paul uses the emphatic construction καί γάρ (kai gar), meaning "for even," to firm up his assertion concerning the greater glory. Here, the use of καί γάρ acts "to introduce a comment intended to clarify and thus further support the argument to which it is added."[26] Paul's placement here of such an emphatic construction serves his argument well. This verse serves to sum up the entire point of verses 7 through 11.[27]

The phrase ἐν τούτῳ τῷ μέρει (en touto meros), meaning "in this part or case," (found only here and in 9:3) refers to the entire preceding remark (that which had glory no longer has it) and introduces the final part of the sentence in which this point is explained.[28]

Paul's inclusion of the adverb οὐ ("not") to the two perfect tense verbs δεδόξασται and δεδοξασμένον presents the reader with an oxymoron.[29] The text literally reads, "The thing (the Mosaic law) that was glorious (δεδόξασται), was not glorious (δεδοξασμένον)." The old covenant was indeed glorious in its own right. However, it cannot compare to the much "greater glory" of the new.

The term translated "greater" comes from the Greek word ὑπερβάλλω (huperballo). This compound word consists of the word βάλλω (ballo) meaning "to throw with force" and the prefix ὑπερ (huper) meaning, as seen in verse 9, "over the top" or "super." The attributes of ὑπερβάλλω prove very similar to περισσεύω. The idea conveyed by this term is that of completely outdoing something or someone. This outdistancing [outthrowing] causes the superior to become incomparable to the inferior.[30]

The English literary device known as a "hyperbole" means "to speak with a force far beyond real life instances." Compared to the rest of the New Testament, 2 Corinthians is rife with the term ὑπερβάλλω and its cognates. In fact, of the 11 times this word (including cognates) is used, more than half occur in 2 Corinthians.[31] Perhaps Paul's opponents claimed that Jesus belonged to the existing (Mosaic) covenant and that no new covenant had come. Such a doctrinal error would have certainly prompted Paul to insist on the surpassing covenant of Christ and the Spirit.

11. For if the ministry being annulled came with glory, that which remains came with much more glory.

In verse 11, Paul wraps up this section of his argument with a final "if . . . then how much more" inquiry. Again, the presence of γὰρ (for) indicates that this verse explains earlier verses (vv. 7, 10).[32] The focus of this verse is temporal. The present participle καταργούμενον (katargeo) expresses continuous action "making ineffective" and refers back to "the law" in verse 10 and so applies to the entire Old Testament, "symbolized by Moses."[33] Thus, Paul boldly declares the entire Mosaic ministry was destined, from the start, for obsoleteness. He presents a strong contrast between the fading (annulled) and remaining glory. As mentioned earlier, the law began to be abolished (or fade) as soon as it was put in force. Thus, the law anticipated the coming of a permanent covenant. Therefore, if the covenant being annulled came[34] διά δόξης (dia doxa), "with glory," πολλῷ μᾶλλον (polus mollon), "much more,"[35] τό μένον ἐν δόξη (meno en doxa), "that which remains in glory." Paul set the present tense participle μένον, meaning "that which is remaining," in direct contrast to καταργούμενον (katargeo), "that which is being annulled."

Some contend that the use of the phrase διά δόξης (dia doxa), meaning "through glory," refers to the accompanying circumstance of the temporal glory and ἐν δόξη (en doxa), or "in glory," refers to the element of the permanent.[36] This line of reasoning must overcome the fact that, even in the immediate context (vv. 7–8), Paul uses ἐν δόξη in reference to both covenants.[37] In the theology of 2 Corinthians, the greater glory is evidenced, above all, in spiritual transformation. Therefore, the living epistles in Corinth testified to the working of the greater glory.

Turner expounds this idea by stating that (perhaps) Paul "took doxa as a symbol for the manifestation of perfected human nature, the most significant symbol known to him for God's perfection."[38] While this idea may go too far, Paul certainly believed that the glory could and should change lives (3:18). After all, the man persecuting the saints beyond measure was never the same after he encountered the surpassing glory.

The old was glorious, but the new, superior covenant has come. This new ministry has its very roots in the old. Therefore, one should seek to understand and appreciate the old covenant. However, the tree now stands in full bloom. Although the soft glow of predawn was wonderful, the noonday sun, in all its brightness, now dominates the sky. In the new age of the Spirit, life and righteousness have outshined death and condemnation. Now the glory of the past has been swallowed up by surpassing glory.

3:12–18

12. Therefore, in the process of holding such amazing hope, we exude great boldness.

Paul breathes in the air of revelation, points back to the immeasurable glory showcased in verses 6 through 11, and states, "Therefore [as a result of the work of Christ] because we have an unsurpassed kind of hope, we exhibit overflowing confidence."

While "faith" (πίστις/pistis) concerns grabbing hold of what God makes presently available, ἐλπίς (elpis), or "hope," connotes an unwavering assurance regarding what God has laid up for a future date. Here, by using "hope," Paul asserts that, in the future, this never waning new covenant glory will shine continually brighter.

The word τοιοῦτος (toioutos) signifies something of a unique class or degree. For example, when Jesus healed a paralyzed man, the people present "marveled and glorified God, who had given such (τοιοῦτος) power to men" (Matt. 9:8 NKJ). The people stood amazed at the never before seen class and degree of power given to Jesus. This high potency hope held forth by Paul belongs to all those in Christ.

In light of such extravagant hope, believers should exude extreme παρρησία (parrhesia), or "confidence," toward God. Many translations have "boldness of speech" here. παρρησία can certainly be used to signify frankness of speaking. However, when it does so, a word connoting speech stands beside it (Mark 8:32; John 7:26, 16:25, 29, 18:20; Acts 2:29, 4:29). Paul's sentence lacks any word pertaining to speech.

Furthermore, the context of his argument pertains to the believer's unhindered relationship with the Lord. The New Testament uses the term παρρησία without accompanying words having to do with speaking, to convey the concept of confidence in accessing God. For example, Paul tells the Ephesian church that "we have boldness and access with confidence through faith in Him" (Eph. 3:12 NKJ). The writer of Hebrews exhorts believers to "come boldly to the throne of grace, that we may obtain mercy and find grace to help in time of need" (Heb. 4:16 NKJ). Thus, the translation "confidence" fits much better with the overall flow of Paul's thought.

13. Now, we are not like Moses, who placed a veil over his face so that the Israelites could not gaze upon the ultimate purpose of that (the law) which is fading away.

The work of Christ has torn the veil formerly sectioning off the Holy of Holies. In addition, all other veils separating believers from the Lord have been thrown aside as useless. Paul tells the church: "We are not like Moses who had to place a covering over his face. [This was necessary because] the Israelites could not see the full purpose of the temporary [fading] glory."

Israel's hard-heartedness rather than God's desire to keep his distance necessitated the veil on Moses face. Indeed, they told Moses "you speak to us, and we will listen. But don't let God speak directly to us, or we will die (Ex. 20:19 NLT)! The entire Bible presents God taking extreme measures in order to draw near, not further away from, those made in his image.

14. But their minds were hardened. For even to this very day when the Old Covenant is being read, the veil remains on, because only in Christ is the veil removed.

Israel failed to realize the purpose or "end" of the old covenant. Although it contained no flaws, God designed the old covenant as a divinely constructed, humanly accessible bridge from Moses to Messiah. With the bridge complete, God's people could walk into a land much greater than the physical Promised Land. Israel misperceived the old covenant as a place of finality. Thus, they missed its τέλος (telos), meaning "end" or "purpose." The English word "telescope" shows the concept of an instrument designed to see to the end of the galaxy. τέλος also speaks of fully completing a purpose.

The first words of Jesus recorded in Scripture are, "I must be about my Father's business" (Luke 2:49). His last words before dying were "It is finished (τέλος)" (John 19:30). When God finishes something, He begins something greater.

While God has removed a series of veils since the time of Moses, the Israelites, "even to this day," see God's Word through densely opaque glass.

15. Even today whenever Moses is read, a veil still drapes over their heart.

The "hardness of mind" displayed in verse 14 has progressed to "covering their hearts" in verse 15. In this phrase, the word translated "upon" comes from the Greek term κεῖμαι (keimai), meaning "to quietly cover."[39] Deception does not come dressed outlandishly, speaking loudly, and working instantly. It appears as a wolf in sheep's clothing, and works undercover at a slow pace. Here, Paul employs the middle voice form κεῖται. This reveals a voluntary cooperation upon the part of the recipient resulting in the translation, "cover themselves with a veil."

Israel did not sit innocently and idly by while deception unexpectedly dropped on them. Instead, what they allowed into their minds eventually reached into their hearts. Paul speaks of this blinding phenomenon in Romans. He presents the problem with fallen humanity, not as ignorance, but rebellion. Indeed, "God shows his anger from heaven against all sinful, wicked people who suppress the truth by their wickedness. They know the truth about God because he has made it obvious to them" (Rom. 1:19 NLT). This serves as the example that the manner with which one hears remains as important as the substance of what one hears. The same Word of God produces both enlightenment in the humble and blindness in the proud.

16. But whenever a person awakes and turns to the Lord, the veil is taken off, cast aside as useless, and abandoned.

Humbling oneself remains both the only and perfect remedy for hardness of heart. Whenever "anyone turns around and walks humbly back to the Lord" the "veil is removed, thrown aside, and abandoned" The word translated "turns to" comes from the Greek term ἐπιστρέφω (epistrepho) meaning " to be awaked and turn around or turn back to." For this reason, it can also mean "to be converted."

John's use of ἐπιστρέφω proves exceptionally relevant to Paul's talk of a vision-impairing veil. He quotes Isaiah saying, "He hath blinded their eyes, and hardened their heart; that they should not see with their eyes, nor understand with their heart, and be converted (ἐπιστρέφω), and I should heal them" (John 12:40 KJV).

The result, according to Isaiah and John, of "awakening, turning, and humbly walking back to God" is "healing." According to Paul, such action results in the veil περιαιρεῖται *(periaireo),* "being taken off, cast aside, and abandoned." The verb περιαιρεῖται stands in the passive construction. This means that God, not the one repenting, takes the veil off. The person remains responsible to turn and walk back to the Lord. The Lord then takes the veil off, casts it aside, and says, "You will never need this again; abandon it forever!"

17. For the Lord is the Spirit, and where the Spirit of the Lord is, there is freedom.

The particular member of the Trinity removing and discarding the veil is the Holy Spirit. In both the tabernacle and temple, the bread of presence in the holy place could only be seen via the light of the lampstand. The bread represents the Word of God and the lampstand the Spirit of God. One can only see the truth of the Word with the light of the Spirit. The Spirit brings ἐλευθερία *(eleutheria),* or "liberty." James uses this word to speak of the "law of liberty": the law governing those under the new covenant (James 1:25, 2:12).

In Romans Paul states, "The law of the Spirit of life in Christ Jesus has made me free (ἐλευθερόω) from the law of sin and death" (Rom. 8:2 NKJ). The manifesting of this law of liberty takes place in believers "who do not walk according to the flesh, but according to the Spirit" (Rom. 8:4 NASB).

18. So all of us with the veil removed from our faces can see the glory of the Lord as in a mirror. And we, by the Spirit of the Lord, are being transformed into that image in ever increasing measures of glory.

Those with unveiled faces can see two things clearly: the glory of the Lord and their need for change. Veils not only keep one from seeing the fullness of God, they distort their own image in the mirror. By beholding the image of God, we "become more fully like Him." The word translated "transformed" comes from the Greek term μεταμορφόω (*metamorphoo*) meaning "to drastically change in form or outward appearance." Most Corinthian readers would have understood the deep philosophical roots of this term, which dates back to Aristotle's concept of "forms." The English word "metamorphosis" comes from this term.

Here, μεταμορφόω takes on the passive verb construction. Thus, the grammar reveals that while "staring contemplatively" into God's glory remains the responsibility of the believer, God alone accomplishes the actual transformation. Even with the case of the "transfiguration" of Jesus, Matthew uses the passive form μετεμορφώθη (Matt. 17:2). Jesus did not "transfigure" himself. Instead, the Spirit did the work. When believers recognize their inward identity, their outward behavior changes dramatically. The Holy Spirit serves as the agent in the process of "allowing God to transform (μεταμορφοῦσθε) every aspect of you by changing the way you think" (Rom. 12:2). In other words, "focus on these things; give yourself fully to them, so that your transformation may be obvious to all" (1 Tim. 4:15).

4:1–18 Living Through Dying

4:1–6

1. Therefore, since we have this ministry by means of God's mercy, we dare not give up.

Paul starts this section with a sentence containing the word translated "mercy." This word comes from the Greek term ἔλεος meaning "to show kindness and goodwill to one in extreme need." No matter how high the Lord lifts up ministers, they must always avoid becoming "shortsighted or blind, forgetting that they have been cleansed from their old sins" (2 Pet. 1:9 NLT). The very word translated "ministry" (διακονία/diakonia) signifies service. Ministry, as Paul details later in this chapter, presents the opportunity to serve others to the point of giving one's life if necessary. No matter the cost, those in ministry can never ἐγκακέω (ekkakeo), or "give up in heart." Once the heart yields to resignation, defeatist actions automatically follow suit.

When writing the churches in Galatia, Paul mentions this very process by saying, "Let us not become worn out to the point of resignation in heart (ἐγκακέω), for at the right time, we will gather a harvest if we do not let go of it all" (Gal. 6:9). The phrase "let go of it all" comes from the Greek word ἐκλύω (ekluo) meaning "to become weary and give up." It is used in sailing lingo to mean, "Let go of the ropes." When one lets go of the ropes, the boat, like the life of one giving up, spins in circles. Oftentimes, engaging in ministry when results appear meager and opposition gigantic makes quitting seem like a fire escape. However, stepping out of one's call proves a door into anguish rather than an escape into ease.

2. We reject all hidden and shameful ways, refusing to walk in deception by distorting the Word of God. Instead, by setting forth the truth, we openly present ourselves to everyone's conscience in the sight of God.

Next, Paul aims his weaponry at the Gnostic concept supremely valuing secret knowledge taught by a select group of enlightened teachers. He presents secretiveness as "shameful" rather than virtuous. Instead of skulking in the dark, Paul preaches with "full disclosure."

He has preached and lived in a manner conducive to a clean "conscience" (συνείδησις/suneidesis). Paul's love for this term stands out in his usage of it nearly twenty times. The gospel is far from secretive. Jesus said of His earthly ministry, "Everyone knows what I teach. I have preached regularly in the synagogues and the temple, where the people gather. I have not spoken in secret" (John 18:20 NLT).

3. If our gospel is veiled, it is veiled from those who are perishing.

The veiled gospel results not from a cloaking desire on God's part, but a satanic blinding of the eyes. If anyone dies while blinded, they will "perish." This word comes from the Greek term ἀπόλλυμι (apollumi) meaning "to be destroyed beyond remedy" and "to be forever separated from an originally designed purpose." Thankfully, God "loved every person with such intensity that He gave His only Son with the end that whoever believes in Him never has to perish (ἀπόλλυμι) but can have never-ending life" (John 3:16). Conversely, "the thief comes only to steal, kill, and destroy (ἀπόλλυμι)" (John 10:10).

4. Satan, the god of this present world system, has blinded the minds of those choosing not to believe so that they might not see the enlightening of the gospel showing the glory of Christ, who is the exact image of God.

The Greek word normally used for "world" does not appear in this phrase. Instead Paul uses the word αἰών (aion) meaning "long period of time." For this reason, some translate the phrase as "god of this age." αἰών can also mean "world." Therefore, either "world" or "age" stand as acceptable translations. Unless they offer it to him, Satan has no authority whatsoever in the lives of believers. However, during this current age, Satan executes authority in the world full of unbelievers.

He can, for this reason, be called both the "god of this age" and "god of this world system." John speaks of this "world system" when he tells believers, "Love not this world nor the things it offers you, for when you love the world, you do not have the love of the Father in you (1 John 2:15 NLT). Of course, sons of God, like their father, should always "love the people trapped in the world system with great intensity"(John 3:16).

Strangely, many blame God for the actions of the god of this world. When Satan unleashes death and destruction, even well-meaning believers falsely accuse God by either asking, "Why did God allow this to happen?" or foolishly stating, "God is in control of everything." Thankfully, the time clock of Satan's rule has reached its final few ticks. Soon, the world will "become the kingdom of our Lord and of his Christ, and he will reign forever and ever" (Rev. 11:15 NLT).

5. For we do not proclaim ourselves, but Christ Jesus as Lord and ourselves your servants in his cause. 6. For God who said, "Let the light outshine darkness" has made his light shine in our hearts for the purpose of revealing to us the glory of God seen in the face of Jesus Christ.

The image the enemy works hardest to distort is that of Christ. All cults hold to and present a blurry, incorrect image of Christ. Leaven of error regarding Jesus leavens the whole lump of one's theology. Satan, the chief leaven sower, knows this well. Even many claiming to have powerful moves of the Spirit sometimes get the focus off of Christ. Rest assured, the Holy Spirit will never move the attention away from Christ. Jesus said of him "He will glorify me" (John 16:14). Paul preaches Christ Jesus the Lord, not himself. Even creation itself preaches Jesus. Just as the Lord spoke physical light into a dark material universe, He now speaks spiritual light into darkened hearts as they look into the peerless face of Jesus Christ.

4:7–18

7. We are now holding this priceless treasure in clay containers. The point of this is to show that the boundless, overflowing, unstoppable power flows from God, not from ourselves.

God has placed his incalculable treasure into containers of clay. Like θήκη forming the chief part of the compound word διαθήκης (covenant) used by Paul in 3:6, θησαυρὸν (thesauros) here means "a receptacle for storing treasure." We see this usage in the English cognate word "thesaurus" signifying "a treasure of words." It's not the box that serves as the source of riches. Many people have a fascination with finding the Old Covenant box or "ark." While thrill seekers look for the box, wise men seek the treasure of the box, not the container itself.

The phrase translated "That the boundless, overflowing, unstoppable power flows from the Lord" is a construction called a genitive of source. Writers employ this grammatical device to show origination. For example, in English one might say, "That hen's eggs" to signify eggs coming from a particular hen. The container serves as the conduit through which God's ability flows, not the source from which it originates. Although conduits remain immensely important, the real value lies in what flows through them. An immensely thirsty person rarely values the faucet above the crystal-clear, cold water flowing out of it. This principle applies to all the gifting of God. None of them belong to the one operating in such giftings. All gifts and callings reside within the laws of stewardship. Thus, everyone will give an account at the judgment seat of Christ regarding the gifting God placed within them.

8. We are pressed from every angle, but not hindered from moving forward; perplexed from every side, but not stepping off the right path and into despair;

In the course of serving the Lord, believers are sometimes "pressured from every angle, but not hindered from moving." The word translated "pressure" comes from the Greek word θλίβω (thlibo) meaning "a pressing from all sides that makes a way narrow" Although the pressures of life sometimes make walking difficult, the Christian need never "cower to pressure that restricts forward movement (στενοχωρέω/stenochoreo)."

The term translated "perplexed" comes from the Greek word ἀπορέω (*aporeo*) meaning "to be uncertain or lacking an answer." It is comprised of a word having to do with "road, path, or way" and the prefix signifying "without." Thus, to experience ἀπορέω means to experience a cloudiness regarding which way to go.

Paul then uses the same word as ἀπορέω with the preposition ἐξ (*ex*), meaning "out of," added as a prefix: ἐξαπορέομαι (*exaporeomai*). While uncertainty sometimes clouds one's path, such uncertainty will never reach a level necessitating stepping out of the right path altogether.

9. hunted down, but not abanonded; knocked down, but not knocked out.

While the enemy actively works to διώκω (*dioko*), or "hunt down to harm" believers, God never "abandons" one of His soldiers on the battlefield. This word comes from the Greek term ἐγκαταλείπω (*eg-kataleipo*) meaning "to leave behind, abandon, or utterly desert." Jesus had already experienced the fullness of horrific abandonment on behalf of all believers. Toward the end of his six hours of unfathomable suffering, he cried out "My God, my God, why have you utterly deserted (ἐγκαταλείπω) me?" (Matt. 27:46). He opened up his back to take away sickness, bled out to take away sin, and cried out to take away abandonment.

Paul turns next to athletic language by saying "we are knocked down, but not knocked out." The word translated "knocked out" comes from the term ἀπόλλυμι discussed earlier in verse 3.

10. At all times we bear in our body the dying of the Lord Jesus so that the life of Jesus may also be manifested in our body.

With the "dying of Jesus in the body," Paul speaks of sacrificing one's physical comfort for the sake of advancing the kingdom. He carries this theme forward throughout 2 Corinthians. Personal preferences, self-serving schedules, and physical ease had no more place in Paul's ministry than they did in the earthly ministry of Jesus.

11. For we constantly live in danger of physical death because of living as examples of Jesus. This makes way for the life of Jesus also manifesting in our mortal body. 12. Thus, while we repeatedly face physical death, this has resulted in eternal life in you.

Laying down one's life for service results in rising up in the supernatural life of God. Paul raised the dead because he died daily to self. Paul carried with him a heavy anointing because he "carried about in the body the dying of Jesus." Only those dead to self stand ready to minster the life of God to others. The Lord's desire to work miracles far outweighs any similar desire in any of His children. His eyes continuously search the earth for those dead to self. For the church to be truly alive, it must first die.

13. Having the same spirit of faith, according to what is written, "I believed; therefore I spoke." In the same way, we believe and speak accordingly.

What keeps Paul selflessly moving forward through persecution, threats of defeat, and temptation to give up? Faith resident in his heart and spoken out of his mouth! He holds forth David's faith in Psalm 116 as an example.

The Psalms burst at their binding with living illustrations of faith. When one reviews the frames of these pictures, an overall pattern emerges. David pours out his struggles to God, God pours in His solution, and David pours forth faith-filled statements of praise. If, under the old covenant, David could have such great faith, how much more should those under a better covenant exude an expectant confidence?

14. We know that He who raised up the Lord Jesus will assuredly, by means of Jesus, raise us up also and present us with you.

15. All this is to benefit you, in order that grace may reach more people by great thanksgiving abounding to the glory of God.

Paul then makes a faith statement of his own regarding the resurrection. No matter how tough things get here in life, a new day lies ahead.

16. For this reason, we never give up in dispair. Even though our mortal body is decaying, our inward man is daily renewed to the degree of amazement.

Although the outward body, until the resurrection, decays, the inner man is "made progressively newer every day." The phrase "made progressively newer" comes from the Greek compound term ἀνακαινόω (anakainoo).

The main part of the word, καινός (kainos) means "new to the degree of amazing." When Jesus spoke "the people were all so amazed that they asked each other, 'What is this? A new (καινός) teaching — and with authority!'" (Mark 1:27 NIV). The old encompasses things corrupted by the fall, but the life-giving power of redemption brings new life to all it touches.

The writer of Hebrews uses καινός when referring to the new covenant (Heb. 8:8, 13). Indeed, although the old bore the pure fingerprint of God, the covenant sealed with the blood of Christ Jesus shouts "new" to a degree producing astonishment. This covenant makes way for believers to "put on the new (καινός) man which was created according to God, in true righteousness and holiness" (Eph. 4:24 NKJ). This new man will live in a "new (καινός) heaven and new (καινός) earth" created by the one who "makes all things new (καινός)" (Rev. 21:1, 5).

The prefixed preposition ἀναα (ana) signifies upward motion. The word also carries the connotation of repetition. Thus, to ἀνακαινόω means to "take up again."[1] Paul wisely applies the word to believers being "made new again [on a daily basis]."

17. For our fleeting, small affliction produces in us an eternal glory that far outweighs any earthly trouble.

In light of what awaits, all trouble, no matter how heavy, appears light as a feather and fleeting as the wind. As an added bonus, temporary opposition produces in us a heavy measure of eternal glory. The word translated "produces" comes from the Greek term κατεργάζομαι (*katergazomai*) meaning "to bring about or produce something via a process." It also has the connotation of "subduing or conquering." This end result of "heavily measured glory" only comes to those who see the process through to victory.

This verb stands in the middle voice. Therefore, a measure of co-operation is required of the believer going through difficulty. Victory comes, not to all who go through trouble, but to those who cooperate with the process until they come out of it. James encourages believers enduring trials by saying, "The testing of your faith produces (κατεργάζεται) strong endurance" (James 1:3). The process has unlimited potential for producing endurance "if you let it" (James 1:4).

18. So we don't fix our gaze on outward circumstances, but on things not seen [with the natural eye]; for the things seen outwardly quickly end, but the things not seen [expect with the eye of faith] remain forever.

Victorious believers do not focus intensely on temporary difficulties associated with the old, corrupted world under Satan's sway. This does not mean they ignore them altogether. Many believers have sand-filled eyes resulting from burying their heads ostrich style at the slightest opposition. The word translated "focus intently" comes from the Greek term σκοπέω (*skopeo*) meaning "to carefully gaze upon and consider." The English word "scope" comes from this term. When a person "scopes something out" they view a situation to the point of carefully studying it. Doctors scope an area of the body in order to carefully examine things.

Believers should acknowledge trouble but must not dwell on the intricacies of it. Doing so only unnecessarily magnifies the scale of difficulty. Adverse circumstances speak loudly, shine brightly, and resist adamantly. However, they do not have real lasting power. The real, eternal power of God requires the eye of faith to see. Enemy armies can easily fill one's field of vision. Nevertheless, the eyes of faith see the Lord's army against which nothing can compete. Seeing with (the eyes of faith) remains inextricably connected to speaking with faith as featured in verse 13.

People both talk about the object of their focus and focus on what they talk about. Those looking with the eyes of faith will report what they see. How they see the enemy will also determine how they view themselves. Some see their enemies as giants and themselves as grasshoppers. Others see themselves as giants and their enemies as grasshoppers.

5:1–21 A Home of Eternal Reconciliation

5:1–9

1. For we know that if our earthy house we live in is taken down, we have a home from God, a house not constructed with human hands, that lasts forever in the heavenly realm.

Paul speaks of believers "strongly desiring to be clothed with our heavenly house." Some translations have "longing to be clothed," while others have "longing to put on." This phrase comes from the middle voice aorist infinitive verb ἐπενδύσασθαι (*ependouomai*) and carries the concept of cooperation. It does not speak of one grabbing clothes and putting them on. Neither does it portray one passively getting dressed by another. Instead, God holds up a new, spiritual body and says, "Step into this; you will love it. These new bodies are "from heaven" (ἐξ οὐρανοῦ/*ex ouranos*)." The genitive construction here speaks of both origination (from) and composition (containing only heavenly essence). The born-again spirits of believers groan to step into their heaven-produced, corruption free bodies!

2. We groan [while in this earthly body] while intensely longing to clothe ourselves with our heavenly dwelling. 3. For, if we cloth ourselves, we will not be found naked.

The inner man regularly sighs deeply for the great things God has in store. Paul places the verb for "groan" (στενάζω/*stenazo*) in the present, active, indicative, first person, plural form στενάζομεν to signify "we are continuously groaning [for our heavenly bodies]." Actually, the entire physical universe "groans (συστενάζει) as in the pains of childbirth" (Rom. 8:22). The poet Coleridge writes, "Earth with her thousand voices praises God." Likewise, the Psalmist notes, "The heavens declare the glory of God; the skies proclaim the work of his hands" (Ps. 19:1 NIV). While all of creation constantly worships the

Lord, it also consistently groans for what lies ahead. Paul speaks polemically regarding the gnostic and Platonic concepts of viewing the physical body as a prison to escape. He asserts that believers should not have a relentless "desire to die and put off our mortal body." Instead, we seek to clothe ourselves with the new.

4. Nevertheless, while we live in this earthly tent we groan under heaviness. This is not due to a desire to die and put off our mortal body. Rather, we seek to clothe ourselves [with the new] so that the mortal might be swallowed up by the God kind of life.

Believers will not float around heaven as a collection of ethereal mist. Paul describes a stepping out of the corruptible body, not into nakedness, but a gloriously designed new body. When this occurs, corruptible bodies "will be swallowed up by the God-kind of life (ζωή/zoe)" (cf. 1 Cor. 15:54).

5. Now He who prepared us for this purpose is God, who has also given us the Spirit as a down payment securing the remaining benefits for future disbursement.

Until that time when believers put on incorruptible bodies, they have, in the indwelling Spirit of God, a down payment (ἀρραβών/arrhabon) or absolute assurance that the day will come. The same Spirit who will transform physical corruption into absolute victory lives inside believers (Rom. 8:11).

6. So we are always confident knowing that while we remain at home in the mortal body, we are not in our permanent home with the Lord. 7. You see, we walk by faith, not by means of sight. 8. We have great confidence and we would rather be absent from the mortal body and be at our permanent home with the Lord. 9. Therefore, we consider it a high honor, weather present or absent, to be well pleasing to Him.

In light of what lies ahead, Paul's statement of confidence while being "absent from the Lord" first appears strange. Why would being away from the Lord produce confidence? The phrase translated "from the Lord" comes from a Greek construction used to express "by means of." The phrase could translate as "by means of the Lord."

The word translated "absent" comes from the Greek verb ἐκδημέω (*ekdemeo*) meaning "to leave home." Thus Paul states, "We always have good cheer; knowing that while currently living in an imperfect body, we are transitioning to the spiritual body by the power of the Lord." The process of physical aging and death may look like loss. However, for the believer, it serves as gradually moving out of the corruptible and into the perfect. Without question, aging and death came through sin and are not God's will. Nevertheless, even in the midst of it, believers have a reason to celebrate. "Though our bodies are dying, our spirits are being renewed every day" (2 Cor. 4:16 NLT). What looks like defeat God turns to victory for those who "walk by faith and not by sight!" In fact, Paul would "rather already have left the corruptible body and been at home in the new body. For this reason, "whether present or leaving, we make it our aim to please the Lord."

5:10–13

10. For every one of us stands exposed before the judgment seat of Christ. There, we will receive our just due for either the good or evil things we have done while living in the mortal body.

Paul says that every believer will be "made known" (φανερόω/*phaneroo*) before the judgement seat (βῆμα/*bema*) of Christ. More specifically, φανερόω means "to make known what has been previously hidden." Nothing will remain hidden during that day. In addition to a judicial seat, βῆμα can mean "a speaker's platform." All believers must approach this seat whereupon Christ will both uncover hidden motives and speak a judgment regarding how they stewarded their lives.

In Paul's day, the wind of gnostic heresy blew around the lie that what one did with the material body proved of little consequence. The

Gnostics claimed to have special, mysterious wisdom. This teaching had crept into the Corinthian church. In 1 Corinthians, Paul speaks of this same judgement event. He says to believers: "You are the temple of God and He lives in you." Sins of the flesh do have bearing at the judgment. Paul contends that what one does in the physical body ($\sigma\tilde{\omega}\mu\alpha$/soma) will have major import at this face-to-face encounter with Christ. If the physical body proves nothing more than a sin-ridden prison house destined for obliteration, God's judgment of believers for their stewardship would appear strange. However, Scripture presents the body as a cherished creation of God.

The psalmist calls the physical body a complex and marvelously made masterpiece (Ps. 139:14). When speaking to the Colossians, Paul carefully asserts that in Jesus, God placed all the fullness of himself into a physical body (Col. 2:9). After it encountered death, the Spirit raised Jesus' body to life forevermore. It did not remain in the tomb! Although affected by sin, the body does not exist as an inconsequential soul-sack exempt from either future usage or excluded from matters of judgment. Instead, Paul teaches believers that the body is made for the Lord, and the Lord cares about our bodies" (1 Cor. 6:13 NLT).

Those at the judgement seat of Christ, unlike the white throne judgement of Revelation, will all enter into heaven. The purpose concerns the rewards, or lack thereof, one will receive from the Lord. Fire will proceed from the judgement seat of Christ testing the genuineness of everyone's life's work. The quality of work depends neither on the amount of talent one possessed not even what they did with it. Instead, the fire reveals and judges the "hidden motives of the heart" (1 Cor. 4:5). Did ego inflation, financial gain, or public praise trump the pure motive of love? If so, no matter how impressive the works appeared to man, God deems it all "wood, hay, and stubble" destined for burning (1 Cor. 3:12–15).

11. Therefore, having this understanding regarding the fear of the Lord, we intensely seek to persuade people [in order to turn them to life]. However, before God we are seen for who we truly are. I trust that we have also been seen as genuine by your consciences.

The Greek word translated "understanding," Εἰδότες (eido), stands in the perfect verb construction. This infuses the verb with the concept of completed action in the past with ongoing effects in the future. In other words, Paul says, "Our knowledge of the fear of the Lord has such a profound, ongoing effect upon us that we seek diligently to persuade people."

12. We are not [like our opponents] relentlessly commending ourselves to you. Instead, we are affording you a real opportunity to be proud of us, so that you can answer those who boast about having a spectacular ministry instead of a pure heart. 13. If we are "crazy," we are crazy for God. If we are in our right minds, it is for your benefit.

He then refers back to talk of his opponents obsession with both giving and seeking recommendations. Paul explains that they boast about surface appearances while he focuses on heart issues. People often enact smoke, mirrors, and all manner of manipulation regarding appearances. Conversely, heart issues cannot remain hidden. The heart need never "boast" (καυχάομαι/kauchaomai). To see its inward content one only need view its outward fruit.

5:14–16

14. For the love of Christ compels us. We remain convinced that if one died for all, that all died. 15. He died for everyone, so that those who live should cease living for themselves but for him who both died and was raised again.

The phrase translated "compels us" comes from the Greek compound word συνέχω (sunecho). The main word ἔχω (echo) means "to have or hold something." The prefixed preposition σύν signifies "together with." In sum, Paul asserts that Jesus has a tight hold on every area of his life. Paul arranged each part of his heart with a hook for Jesus to latch onto. He sees this level of commitment as obligatory, not optional. How can he not live for the one who paid his sin debt through death? The opposite of this can be seen in those who remain "entangled with the affairs of this life and cannot please their commanding officer" (2 Tim. 2:4).

16. So that we no longer evaluate people from a selfish vantage point. Even though we may have known Christ as a mere human, yet we know him that way no longer.

Now that he has moved into newness of life, Paul no longer evaluates people from a merely natural perspective. Believers seeing others through the eyes of the Lord treat people with true love. Gifts in others often lie hidden under multiple layers of junk. One looking with natural eyes sees only hindrances and failures. God, on the other hand, sees immense potential. Believers looking through the eyes of Jesus are "touched" with the weaknesses present in others (Heb. 4:15). Viewing others through the lens of self-centeredness magnifies their weaknesses as sources of irritation rather than reasons for compassion. Additionally, seeing others from a selfish position filters all they do and say through the lens of "How will they benefit me?"

Conversely, the divine love "widely and deeply disbursed in our hearts by the Holy Spirit" (Rom. 5:5) is never "self-seeking" (1 Cor. 13:5). This heart-snare advertises itself whenever its victims speaks. Such speech takes on three forms: faultfinding, boasting, and deceptive flattery. Jude sums this up nicely by stating, "they live only to satisfy their own desires. They find fault, brag loudly, and flatter others to get what they want" (Jude 1:16). At one point, Paul even viewed Christ according to a natural viewpoint (κατὰ σάρκα/kata sarx). Paul saw Jesus as a mere man from Nazareth claiming divine inspiration upon his preaching. However, once the light of God seen in the face of Jesus Christ shone upon Paul's heart, he saw Jesus as "Lord."

5:17–21

17. Therefore anyone who is in Christ is a new creation. The old passed away; look everything has been made new.

Here, Paul describes the work of the new birth with several truth heavy words. If anyone, regardless of their past, comes into Christ they are a "new creation." This phrase comes from the Greek words καινός (*kainos*), which could be translated "newness to a startling degree," and κτίσις (*ktisis*), meaning "creation" or "the sum of everything created." The regenerated believer is not the same person cleaned up, but a strikingly new person in every aspect of their inner being.

The word "old things" comes from the Greek word ἀρχαῖα (*archaios*) meaning "ancient" or "long standing." The term "passed away" comes from the Greek verb παρέρχομαι (*parerchomai*) meaning "to come to an end" or "disappear altogether." The old way has existed collectively since the fall of humanity and in the individual's life since birth. However, in Christ, it has ended and disappeared!

18. All things accomplished in the new creation spring from God, who reconciled us to Himself through Jesus Christ. And He gave us the ministry of reconciliation.

Some translate verse 18 as "All things are of God." However, the translation "all the things [regarding the new creation] are accomplished by God" works much better with the grammar present in both the verse itself and the verse preceding it. The Greek phrase πάντα ἐκ τοῦ θεοῦ (*panta ek theos*), "all things are of God," is an example of the genitive of agency.

This construction reveals the agent accomplishing a thing. The word translated "reconciled" comes from the Greek term καταλλάσσω (*katallasso*). This term often found usage in financial transactions for reconciling an overdrawn account with currency equal to the debt owed. Many fallen truly owed a debt they miserably lacked the ability to repay. No currency exists in earth or heaven with enough value to reconcile the account. Only the priceless blood of Jesus satisfied the debt and brought reconciliation to the account.

Peter expounds upon the same concept by telling the church, "You were not redeemed with corruptible things, like silver or gold, from your aimless conduct received by tradition from your fathers, but with the precious blood of Christ" (1 Pet. 1:18–19 NKJ). During His earthly ministry, God was busy in Christ, not "carefully keeping an account" (λογίζομαι/*logizomai*) of peoples sins, but instead reconciling the account of humanity.

19. For God was in Christ reconciling the world to Himself, not keeping a careful record of and handing down judgment for their sins. And He has placed within us [entrusted us] with the message of reconciliation. 20. So, we are Christ's ambassadors; God is making an appeal through us. On behalf of Christ we implore people [saying] "Be reconciled to God!"

Now, God has committed to those reconciled the ministry of telling others that their account has been cleared. The term translated "committed" comes from the Greek term τίθημι (*tithemi*) meaning "to set in place." It carries the aspect of one setting a thing in place with someone he trusts. Paul uses the same word to describe God "placing" the ministry gifts within the body of Christ (1 Cor. 12:28). The Lord placed the responsibility of the ministry of reconciliation in a place He trusts: His body.

Telling others that God has paid the sin debt does not mean that people have no need to repent and believe the gospel. Jesus certainly paid the price for all. Nevertheless, not all will be saved. Love always makes the gifts of God available. However, the exercise of faith appropriates the already available gift to the lives of those believing. This principle jumps from the page in the words "God loved the world with such intensity that He gave His only begotten Son. So that whoever believes in Him does not have to perish, but can enjoy everlasting life" (John 3:16). Love gives, faith receives. Thus, because love stands higher than faith, "you place yourself in a greater state of joy while giving" (Acts 20:35).

21. For the one who never sinned was made to be sin [by taking on the penalty for the entirety of sin] for us [on our behalf as our substitute] so that we have the opportunity to become the righteousness of God in Him [Christ].

This law of faith and love finds further expression in verse 21. Paul exclaims that Jesus "knew no sin." The word translated "knew" comes from the Greek term γινώσκω (*ginosko*) meaning "knowing through personal interaction." This term finds usage as a euphemism for sexual intercourse. The omnipotent Son of God certainly had an awareness of the reality of sin. In fact, He left heaven for the purpose of dealing with the problem. However, He "never had any personal interaction with sin." Amazingly, during Christ's time of suffering, God "put upon him the totality of sin." He took the full measure of every wicked deed committed from Adam's first bite of forbidden fruit to the very moment He died. Furthermore, He bore the weight of all sins committed from that time forward.

God did not simply grab a passing thought of mercy, wave a magic wand, and arbitrarily make the penalty for sin disappear. He always keeps His word; including the promise to Adam that "If you eat [disobey], you will die." Sin evoked the ferocious wrath of God upon all of humanity. Denying this truth requires leaping over a mountain of scriptures.

This, however, in no way diminished the love of God. In Christ, the love and justice of God fully collided when the "Son of His love" (Col. 1:13) drank the cup containing the fierceness of God's wrath to the very last drop. In this single event, one witnesses, at once, the full manifestation of both the "goodness and severity of God" (Rom. 11:22). Now, no person need ever drink from the dreadful cup again (Isa. 51:22). A single drop of His blood cleaned, to a crystalline clarity, the entire ocean of sin. All former accounts hopelessly in the negative now lie filled to overflowing with righteousness.

This righteousness far exceeds the righteousness of the keepers of the law. The old covenant sacrificial system merely pushed, by faith, the penalty for sin forward to the day of Christ. Not a single priestly animal offering contained, in itself, any power to redeem. Only those lambs offered in faith regarding the coming Lamb of God had power to save. In the garden, God did not say "it (a ritual, good work, or animal sacrifice) will pay the penalty for sin and crush the serpent," but "He" (the person of Christ). From moments after Adam's fall to the unfolding of the new heavens and new earth, salvation was, is, and always will be solely through faith in the work of Jesus Christ. One does not earn this right standing by keeping enough rules. Instead, one receives it as a gift made available through the obedience of Christ.

Therefore, anyone rejecting the sacrifice, no longer draped in the shadows of the priestly system, has no excuse before God. In truth, "no [other] sacrifice for sins is left. There is only the terrible expectation of God's judgment and the unfathomable fire" (Heb. 10:26–27). However, those accepting the gift, become the very righteousness of God. This standing equates to nothing blocking one's relationship with the Lord. Paul uses the subjunctive mood for the verb signifying "made." Thus, the verse reads, "might be made the righteousness of God." The subjunctive mood portrays a strong possibility, but not absolute certainty. This particular verb mood finds expression all over the New Testament. The reality of free will accounts for such high usage of the subjunctive grammatical device. God's love makes all the blessings available.

These blessings convey an absolute certainty, expressed via the indicative verb mood. However, faith must reach out and grab hold of what the hand of love extends. God desires that people take it, Satan cannot stop it, and free will either accepts or rejects it. The subjunctive here brings the argument of universalism (the belief that the sacrifice of Christ will eventually save everyone whether they accept it in this life or not) to a bone crunching halt. The passage does not say, "He who knew no sin became sin, that we are the righteousness of God in Him." Instead, it states, "that we have the opportunity to become."

We find this principle expressed before Israel entered the Promised Land. God's love had secured the land for Israel's taking. The Lord had Moses explain — his words took up several chapters — both the curses associated with disobedience and the blessings connected to obedience. In order to provide a concrete reminder, he instructed six of the twelve tribes to stand on a certain mountain while proclaiming the curses. Conversely, he told the other six tribes to stand on an opposing mountain while reading the blessings. There, in between, stood the valley of decision. One only crosses this valley to one side or the other by exercising either faith or unbelief. Finally, the word came forth saying, "This day I call the heavens and the earth as witnesses against you that I have set before you life and death, blessings and curses. Now choose life, so that you and your children may live" (Deut. 30:19 NIV). Paul explains that believers have the ministry of standing on the mountain saying, "The sacrifice has been offered. The price has been paid. The way stands open. Now, be reconciled to God. Choose life!"

6:1–18 Genuine Relationship

6:1–7

1. We then, working together with God urge you to not accept the grace of God in vain. 2. For He says, "At the right time I heard you. In the day of salvation, I helped you." Pay attention, now is the right time. Now is the day of salvation. 3. We order our lives in a way that provides no fuel for offense that would discredit our ministry. 4. Instead, we stand as God's ministers in everything we do. We endure opposition, tough times, calamities,

Paul reminds the Corinthians that, no matter how great the magnitude of God's grace, one can receive it "in vain." This phrase comes from the Greek word κενός (kenos) meaning "empty" and "without reaching a predetermined goal or result." After unrolling a list of character traits believers must increasingly exemplify, Peter strikes this same chord by saying, "If you possess these qualities in increasing measure, they will keep you from being ineffective and unproductive in your knowledge of our Lord Jesus Christ" (2 Pet. 1:8 NIV). One can have a beautiful portrait of accurate knowledge and fail to embody a single brush stroke.

While in heaven, Jesus knew every intricacy of God's plan to save humanity. However, he had to rise up from the throne, step down to earth, and die. The use of the word "working" in this verse amplifies the concept of action. Speaking of his own ministry, Paul tells the Corinthians in an earlier letter, "[God's] grace was not without results (κενός). For I have worked harder than any of the other apostles; yet it was not I but God who was working through me by his grace" (1 Cor. 15:10 NLT).

In addition to working zealously, effective workers exercise great care to avoid the ministry-killing virus of scandal.

5. beatings, imprisonments, riots, exhausting work, nights without sleep, and fastings. 6. We do this with purity, with

knowledge, with patience, with kindness, by the Holy Spirit, with sincere love.

Paul then runs down a list of attributes exuding from truly qualified ministers. The pairing of the Holy Spirit with the love of God often occurs in Paul's writings. The Spirit first "pours God's love to overflowing in our hearts" and keeps the level high as believers regularly "commune with the Holy Spirit" (Rom. 5:5; 2 Cor. 13:14). Similarly, Jude proclaims that by "praying in the Spirit, you keep yourselves in the love of God" (Jude 1:20–21).

7. By the word of truth, by the power of God; through the armor of righteousness on the right and on the left,

Some translators use "on the right hand and on the left hand" in verse 7 as a reference to both offensive and defensive weaponry. For example, "We use the weapons of righteousness in the right hand for attack and the left hand for defense" (2 Cor. 6:7 NLT). The original language does not include any word related to "defense." Roman soldiers did, however, carry a short, leaf-shaped blade called a *pugio* on their left side. They used this weapon, not for defense, but close in, quick killing.[1]

While many translators include the word "hand" in this verse, the term does not appear in Greek. Nevertheless, including "hand" in a translation does have a strong historical basis. Greek and subsequently every Roman soldier carried his shield with the left hand while wielding his weapons with the right.

Also, Paul may refer to one's right and left side of the body. Both the Greek "phalanx" and Roman "tortoise" formations required an interlocking of shields necessitating the covering of those on both the outer most left and right flanks of a unit. Occasionally, someone puts forth the foolish assertion that there is no defensive function to the armor of God. If by "defensive" one envisions a fear-fueled retreat, such a contention rings true. However, while forwardly advancing the kingdom on earth, believers must, at times, defend themselves against the onslaught of the enemy. Satan does not instantly lie down and quit whenever threatened by the work of God. In response to a barrage of burning missiles, one must learn to skillfully hold up the shield of faith (Eph. 6:16). Satan both accurately knows and mercilessly attacks vulnerable spots in the lives of believers. Remaining aware of any unprotected areas represents wisdom and not, as some would assert, a lack of faith. Someone who has gained victory over an addiction to alcohol proves not his faith, but his ignorance, by witnessing in a bar.

Of course, Christ sets people forever free from enslaving behaviors. In Christ, the addict no longer remains an addict. He is not the same person on a path to freedom, but a brand new creation.

6:8–13

8. [We continue to minister] through [others showing] honor or dishonor, bad reports or good reports. [Some even call us] deceivers, yet we are genuine. 9. We are considered by some as unknown, although we are well known. We face death, but look, we live on. We have been beaten, but not put to death.

In verse 8, Paul begins again to defend himself against the accusations of his opponents. Paul's biting, acerbic sarcasm comes across loud and clear by reaching back to verse 4, grabbing the words "revealing ourselves as true ministers of God," and attaching them here. The resultant translation comes through as, "We remain true ministers of God if others honor or despise us, if they speak truth or lies regarding us. We are genuine, but they call us fake." Paul has no issue being unknown to the masses of people. Fame has never occupied his aim. He seeks to make known not himself, but Christ. Furthermore, the powers of hell both know and fear him. (Acts 19:15).

10. We experience grief, but we always rejoice. We experience financial challenges, but we make many rich. We hold tightly to nothing [in this world], but we posses all things. 11. Oh Corinthians, we have spoken openly to you, and our hearts remain open to you as well.

Paul's comments about material wealth have caused some to erroneously believe that he glorified poverty. Representing Paul as a poor beggar does not correspond to the reality of his life. A poor beggar does not travel the world on a regular basis, give generously to others, and personally support the missionary journeys of his apprentice. Paul, like Jesus, never chased after earthly riches. Instead, he poured all of this time, talents, and treasures into advancing the kingdom of God. He walked on both sides of the Matthew 6:33 coin. This means that, true to the promise of God, his "seeking first the kingdom" resulted in "all the other [material wealth] things being added to him." Although Paul had money, money did not have Paul. He understood that "Those who use the things of the world should not become attached to them. For this world as we know it will soon pass away" (1 Cor. 7:31 NLT). Paul also realized that, in the course of advancing the gospel, "[The Lord] delights in the prosperity of His servant" (Ps. 35:27 NASB). His life became, not a pool of hording, but a river of giving and receiving.

12. We are not withholding our affection from you, but you have restricted your love. 13. Now, I am requesting something from you as I would my own children. Open up [your hearts] to us.

Paul then appeals for the church to open up to him. Their love for him has become "restricted." This word comes from the Greek term στενοχωρέω (stenochoreo) meaning "to crowd out" or "confine." Like the parable of the sower, certain things have crept in, grown up, and begun crowding out the good things Paul planted in them.

6:14–18

14. Stop pairing yourselves up with unbelievers. For how can righteousness and lawlessness link up together in partnership? What close relationship does light have with darkness?

Paul uncovers the deadly roots crowding out their love. The "super apostles" have superimposed worldly standards of success onto the church. A love for this world has spread like a voracious weed around their hearts. The word translated "unequally yoked" comes from the Greek term ἑτεροζυγοῦντες (*heterozugeo*) meaning "mismatched" or "the wrong partner." The word finds usage in placing a pair of oxen into the same harness. If they pull in opposite directions, the yoke will crack, the animals will experience injury, and the work will go undone. Writers used a similar term when referring to a mismatch of soldiers. An army with a divided infantry cannot possibly win a single battle. The verb γίνεσθε (*ginomai*) sits in the imperative middle second person plural construction. This translates as the command, "You all stop allowing yourselves to be mismatched with unbelievers!" Jesus has called his church to fiercely love unbelievers.

This kind of love requires the forming of friendships. Jesus Himself was often called "a friend of sinners." The Bible also says that "friendship with the world means you are an enemy of God" (James 4:4). This seeming contradiction really exists as a paradox rather than a contradiction.[2] Believers remain saddled with a responsibility to develop friendships with nonbelievers while, at the same time, never connecting to the world's value system.

Nevertheless, fellowship differs from friendship. The term translated "friend" comes from the Greek word φίλος (*philos*) meaning "to be friendly to one" or "to seek to go to another." On the other hand, the word translated "fellowship" here comes from the Greek term μετοχή (*metoche*) meaning "deep mutual sharing and participation." It conveys an uncommon vulnerability. The same meaning exists, in an even deeper level in the word κοινωνία (*koinonia*), translated "fellowship." In life's relationships requiring a great deal of give and take undergirded by firm belief in Scripture, one must not enter into agreements with unbelievers. Preachers have often correctly appealed to this passage when discouraging believers from marrying unbelievers.

15. What mutual agreement can stand between Christ and the devil? What does a believer have in common with an unbeliever?

Light and darkness, Christ and the devil, faith and unbelief, these things can never comingle. Believers do not just have a connection with God; He takes up personal residence inside them.

16. And what agreement does the temple of God have with idols? For we are the temple of the living God. As God has said, "I will live in them, and will walk among them. I will be their God and they will be my people."

The word translated "temple" comes from the Greek word ναός (*naos*). This word means specifically the most holy parts of a temple. In Greek pagan temples, it spoke of the room where the temple's chief idol resided. The Septuagint uses the term to specify the holy place and Holy of Holies and not the entire temple complex. In both pagan and godly settings, it refers to the place where either god or God dwells in manifest power. The thought of God sharing His most holy place with idols causes the universe to shudder.

17. For this reason, step away from those kind of relationships with believers and separate yourselves from them, says the Lord. Stop touching what is unclean; and I will welcome you. 18. "And I will be your Father and you will be my sons and daughters," says the Lord Almighty.

Therefore, to experience the Lord's manifest presence, the church must break free from ungodly associates. One cannot hope to have intense fellowship with the Father while casually fellowshipping with idols. This separation must be so stringent as to not even touch certain unclean things. The term translated "unclean" or "filthy" comes from the Greek compound word ἀκάθαρτος (*akathartos*). The main part of the word, κάθαρα (*kathara*) means "what is cleansed or purified." The English word "cathartic" meaning "to purge oneself" comes from this term. The prefix α signifies "without." The ἀκάθαρτος thing refuses to undergo the purging process and remains perpetually filthy.

The passage Paul quotes here does not appear in the Old Testament. Some have hypothesized that it refers to an ancient Hebrew hymn.

7:1-16 Profitable Sorrow

7:1-4

1. Therefore, because we possess all these promises, dear friends, let us cleanse ourselves from everything that contaminates body and spirit. And let us keep moving toward completion of holiness out of reverence for God. 2. Open your hearts to us. We have wronged no one, we have led no one astray, we have exploited no one.

Although exceptionally helpful, none of God's Word came pre-loaded with chapters and verses. Occasionally, the editors end and begin chapters at glaringly artificial junctures. Here lies a perfect example. Paul continues, uninterrupted with the flow of thought, regarding our separation from the world and to God. He speaks about things that can defile the flesh and the spirit.

Some teach that a believer's sprit can never be defiled, no matter how they live. A few go so far as to argue that sins involving the body have no real consequence. Such error comes from a failure to understand the difference between "distinction" and "separation."

A person's body, soul, and spirit, are obviously distinct from one another. One's soul is not the same thing as one's spirit. Making such a proper distinction between soul and spirit has helped believers walk in a much greater measure of victory. For example, knowing the difference between believing with one's spirit and soul allows one to not fall prey to Satan's lie that "because that doubting thought came up, you are not in faith." The knowledge that faith is birthed in the spirit allows one to fend off doubtful thoughts as the mind continues the process of renewal.

Nevertheless, believers dare not move to the other pole of extremity: separation. The tri-part design of humans does not equate to three separate parts. For example, the separating of the soul from the body results in death, and what one does with the body affects the spirit and soul and vice versa. For example, worry, caused by wrong thinking in the soul, causes the body to get run down. Similarly, when one engages in sexual sin, it has an effect upon the soul.

Sanctification in both the Old and New Testaments involves the working of God and the believer. Several scriptures speak of the Lord sanctifying those who believe. Other verses speak of "sanctifying yourself." Without God's grace, sanctification remains totally impossible. However, the idea of perpetually living a carnal life while claiming sanctification remains a myth. The phrase translated "perfecting holiness" comes from the Greek word ἐπιτελοῦντες (epiteleo) meaning "seeing a process or design through to completion." Here, the participle stands in the active, third-person, plural construction. This means believers must take an active part in sticking with the process of sanctification. Passionately reaching for God's sanctifying grace while tightly gripping the idols of this world mirrors believing for healing of lung cancer while chain smoking.

3. I do not say this in order to condemn you. I have said before that you remain in our hearts to die and live with you.

After speaking such strong correction, Paul reminds the Corinthians that fatherly correction and not castigating condemnation spurs his exhortation. He does not lecture inferiors from an aloof position. Instead, his heart abides with them in life or death.

Walking through life with another produces a level of credibility not attained by outside "experts," no matter how well versed in a subject they may be. Jesus forever displayed the ultimate representation of this principle. Rather than shout commands from a fiery cloud, he stepped into this sin-stained realm as a human. He purposely experienced the full spectrum — minus disobedience to God — of human life. He subjected himself to parental authority, every conceivable temptation, personal rejection at its darkest level, off-the-charts unjust persecution, and a horrific physical death. This eternally destroys the lie that it's easy for Him to say that, He's divine. God doesn't know what it's like.

4. I have great confidence regarding you; I speak very highly of you. I am greatly encouraged. I am overflowing with joy despite all our affliction.

In spite of Paul's fiery speech, he has great confidence in the church at Corinth. Like any great mentor, Paul invests correction into those who have potential to actually improve. Their setbacks do not negate the positive progress the church made.

Jesus takes this approach when addressing the churches in Revelation. He tells them, "Those whom I love, I rebuke and discipline. So be earnest and repent" (Rev. 3:19 NIV). Along with rebuking them, He affirms His confidence in them by commending the churches. Believers ought not despair when the Lord speak a word of discipline. Yielding to such instruction produces great results. Indeed, "No discipline is enjoyable while it is happening — it's painful! But afterward there will be a peaceful harvest of right living for those who are trained in this way" (Heb. 12:11 NLT). Actually, believers should exercise concern if they never hear words of correction. For "the Lord disciplines those he loves, and he chastens each one he accepts as his child. Who ever heard of a child who is never disciplined by its father?" (Heb. 12:6–7 NLT).

7:5–16

5. When we came to Macedonia, we couldn't rest. We encountered harassment wherever we went — conflicts on the outside and alarm within. 6. However, God who comforts the discouraged, comforted us by the arrival of Titus. 7. In addition to his arrival bringing us comfort, so did him telling us how he was comforted by visiting you. When he informed us about your intense desire to see me, your sorrow [for what happened between us], and your concern for me, I rejoiced even more.

In several places of this portion of chapter 7, Paul mentions the interaction involving Titus and the church in Corinth. Paul's discussion here reiterates aspects of this relationship dynamic already dealt with in chapter 2. Nevertheless, several verses in this section merit comment.

8. Even though I caused you sorrow with my letter, I do not regret it, though at first I was sorry. For I realize that the letter caused you temporary sorrow.

In verses 8 through 11, Paul details the important concept of godly sorrow. He starts by saying he "is not sorry for sending the letter of severe correction." His reason for this reveals a clear distinction between godly and ungodly sorrow. In these four verses, Paul uses various forms of the verb λυπέω (*lupeo*), meaning "to have intense pain or deep sorrow," seven different times. The first trait of godly sorrow exposed by Paul concerns its temporary nature. While worldly sorrow keeps people pressed down indefinitely, godly sorrow lasts for a brief time.

9. Now I rejoice that I sent it, not because it made you sorrowful, but because that sorrow caused you to repent. For you were made to experience godly sorrow and were not harmed by us in any way.

Furthermore, godly sorrow "produces not despair, but repentance." The word translated "repentance" comes from the Greek term μετάνοια (*metanoia*) meaning "to turn one's direction" or "change one's mind." Some contend that repentance means merely a change of mind. Indeed, as shown above, μετάνοια does mean "a change of mind" or "a change in patterns of thinking." Nevertheless, in Scripture, this change of thought always produces a changed lifestyle.

10. For godly sorrow produces repentance resulting in salvation. This kind of sorrow leaves one with no regret. However, the sorrow of the world gives birth to death.

In the verses immediately below, Paul commends the Corinthians for their change in actions resulting from their changed mind. This change of direction caused them to gain rather than "suffer loss (ζημιόω/*zemioo*)." James, like Paul, lists a chain reaction of results ending in death by saying, "When desire has conceived, it gives birth to sin; and sin, when it is full-grown, brings forth death." (James 1:15 NKJ). Here, Paul asserts that "worldly sorrow leads to indefinite despair. Then, this despair weighs one down with harmful condemnation. Finally, it gives birth to death ($\theta\acute{\alpha}\nu\alpha\tau\sigma\varsigma$/thanatos)."

Conversely, godly sorrow lasts only a brief time, produces changes in mind and lifestyle, and gives birth to salvation ($\sigma\omega\tau\eta\rho\acute{\iota}\alpha$/soteria) [all the benefits of the work of Christ]. The writer of Hebrew echoes this sentiment when he tells believers, "No discipline is enjoyable while it is happening — it's painful! But afterward there will be a peaceful harvest of right living for those who are trained in this way" (Heb. 12:11 NLT).

11. Observe what this godly sorrow produced in you: such diligence, such attention to clear yourselves, such indignation, such alarm, such intense desire to see me, such zeal, such readiness to hand out justice! In everything you proved yourselves to be pure in this matter.

Paul encourages the church to "Look at [review] the great things this sorrow has produced in you." One fruit of note in the list is what the *King James Version* translates as "revenge." Other versions have "indignation" or "vengeance" here. This word comes from the Greek term $\dot{\epsilon}\kappa\delta\acute{\iota}\kappa\eta\sigma\iota\varsigma$ (ekdikesis) meaning "to hand out justice." This could find application in either ensuing justice on behalf of the oppressed (Luke 18:7) or enacting righteous judgment against sinful behavior in a church setting. In light of Corinth's former issue with taking the ostrich approach to sexual immorality, Paul almost certainly had the later application in mind.

12. Therefore, although I wrote to you, I did not do so concerning the one who did the wrong or who received the wrong done. I wrote so that in the sight of God you could witness your own loyalty to us. 13. This caused us to be encouraged. In addition to our own encouragement, we were especially glad to see how happy Titus was, because you all refreshed his spirit. 14. I have boasted to him concerning you, and you have not put me to shame. Just as I spoke the truth to you

about everything else, so also our boasting to Titus proved true. 15. Now his care for you is greater than ever as he recalls how you obeyed his instruction and respectfully welcomed him. 16. I rejoice because I have total confidence in you all.

8:1–24 The Grace of Giving

8:1–9

1. Now, dear brothers and sisters, we want you to know about the grace God has given to the churches in Macedonia.

Paul transitions into the subject of financial giving and receiving. He regularly uses the phrase, "Now, we want you to know (Γνωρίζομεν δὲ ὑμῖν/gnorizo de humin)" to signal a change in focus. Paul begins by bringing onto center stage the Macedonian churches. Macedonia refers to the region in the north mainland of Greece. During his second missions endeavor, Paul planted the churches of Philippi, Berea, and Thessalonica in this area. An extraordinary centuries long rivalry existed between Macedonia and the rest of Greece, including the southern peninsula of Achaia wherein sits Corinth. Paul appeals to the seeds of this rivalry embedded in Corinthian society by commending the lavish offering[1] given by the Macedonian churches. It's as if he tacitly says, "You certainly don't want the Macedonians to out give you."

The Macedonians had two challenges: some form of unspecified severe opposition and an attack on their finances. They responded to the first line of opposition with an overflowing, supernatural joy. They launched a rapid, bold, and precise counterattack regarding their financial situation. Their handling of the assault reveals the wisdom of fighting back in kind.

For example, when the enemy launches missiles of division a precise counterstrike works best. If he seeks to plant unity killing thoughts about a fellow believer or church leader, the wise Christian will begin praying for the very person those demonic thoughts attempt to undermine. When the devil purposes to plant distrust by means of gossip, the best defense comes in the form of speaking highly of those targeted by the arrows of evil speaking.

This divinely-designed principle also works regarding finances. Believers under financial assault do themselves a grave disservice by hiding in a bunker of doubt until "things get better financially." The path out of the money draining maze of poverty is always marked "giving."

2. That, while being tested with serious opposition they exhibited overflowing joy. Although they had [a trial of] severely deep financial challenges, they responded with rich [financial] generosity.

These churches gave outrageously in the midst of an economic crisis. The phrase translated "deep poverty" comes from the two Greek words, κατά (kata) meaning "down," and βάθους (bathos) meaning "extra deep." These believers had reached the ocean floor of financial trouble. At the bottom of the barrel, they faced a colossal test (δοκιμή/dokime) of character. δοκιμή means "a test that, if passed produces character." Paul uses this word when telling the churches in Rome to rejoice at trials because "we know that they help us develop endurance. And endurance develops strength of character (δοκιμή)" (Rom. 5:3–4 NLT).

The Macedonians passed the twofold character test with flying colors. The test concerned giving two things they currently had instead of either waiting for more or complaining of lack. They had an abundance of joy and a small amount of money. Rather than give "once their ship came in," they gave what little they had with over-the-top joy. This caused their ship of prosperity to begin sailing. Like Jesus with the widow's mite, Paul called their monetarily small gift "abounding."

3. For I personally attest that they gave as much as they had the ablility to give, they even gave far beyond their ability. They did this of their own choosing [they didn't require any spurring on by me]. 4. They actually repeatedly begged us to take up an offering to give to the saints [their fellow believers in Jerusalem]. 5. And they exceeded our expectation in this. First, they gave themselves to the Lord, and then to us according to the will of God.

God never measures the size of gifts according to dollar amount. The Lord considers the percentage one gives compared to what one possesses. Jesus still watches at the treasury. He counts the gift of the person with ten dollars giving nine as of far greater value than the one with a million dollars giving away one hundred thousand.

The Macedonians went so far as to repeatedly pester Paul to take up an offering for the church in Jerusalem. Those constantly asking for an opportunity to give an offering surely understood the power of giving and receiving! The Macedonians gave not just their money but themselves. A person's money represents an extension of themself. One's bank balance provides an accurate measurement of what one values. In fact, if Jesus doesn't have a person's money, he certainly does not have their heart.

6. As a result, we urged Titus [to return to you and] to bring to encourage you to fulfill the work of grace [regarding your giving] that he helped you start.

The Corinthians have an established, healthy working relationship — including the taking up of offerings — with Titus. For this reason, Paul plans on sending him back to finish the fundraising project already in progress. Regarding fundraising, church leaders should never underestimate the power of trust. Concerning offerings: people respond well to a gifted speaker; they respond better to someone they trust; and they respond best to a gifted speaker they trust.

7. Even as you abound in everything you already do — in faith, in gifted speakers, in knowledge, and in all sincerity, and in the love we sparked in you — make it a point to also excel in this grace of giving.

When exhorting the Corinthians to change, Paul uses the technique modeled by Jesus in Revelation 2 and 3 of praising strengths prior to pointing out weaknesses. He begins by commending them for their "faith, gifted speakers, knowledge, and zeal" — if the Corinthians were anything at all, they were zealous. Regarding the moving of the

Spirit, they "came behind in no spiritual gift" (1 Cor. 1:7). However, a healthy church thrives in all six aspects of functionality mentioned in Acts 2:44 through 47: teaching God's Word, prayer, fellowship, worship, evangelism, and financial giving. Thus, Paul urges them to allow the fire present in those areas to consume any stinginess regarding finances and burn bright for the kingdom. Money occupies a major section on the field of life, the words of Jesus, and the pages of Scripture. Believers refusing to surrender their finances to the kingdom unwittingly exclude God from a massive segment of their lives.

Some claim that "tithing isn't for today." If, by this they mean, "we are under a better covenant and should give far more than ten percent," the statement has great value. However, such banter most often truly means "I am free, under the new covenant, from financial obligation to the church." They pray, study the Bible, fast, and prophesy without fully letting go their finances. Exercising precise care on several vital areas while gravely neglecting another, equally important sector equates to disaster in nearly any life endeavor. A sports team perfecting the elements of its offense while saying, "We just don't believe playing defense is for today" will surely lose.

Paul challenges them, not to give a little, but to "abound in the spirit-empowered lifestyle of giving." The word translated "abound" comes from the Greek term περισσεύω (perisseuo) meaning "overflowing abundance," "overflow," and "far more than enough." Greeks used this word to refer to someone extremely prominent and rich. Interestingly, Paul uses the term twice, with two different forms, in this single sentence. In the former instance, he employs the present, active indicative verb form. This means "you are currently and consistently exhibiting overflow regarding faith, gifted speakers, knowledge, and zeal." In the latter part of the verse, Paul places the same verb in the present, active, subjunctive form. This means the overflow remains a possibility to either grasp or let slip away. In sum, he says "in the same manner you have with other spiritual disciplines, take advantage of the life of abundance present in giving and receiving finances!"

8. I am not speaking this as an order, but I am testing, by comparing it with the zeal of others, the genuineness of your love.

Paul explains that he is not "ordering" them to give. Instead, he seeks to determine the quality of their love. One values what one loves. How one spends money paints a vivid picture of one's hierarchy of value. The word translated "testing" comes from the Greek term δοκιμάζω (*dokimazo*) meaning "carefully examine, put to the test, and declared approved or rejected." This word often found usage in testing precious metals. When gold, for example, is placed into the fire, any impurities escape out of the metal in the form of dross. The gold remaining after removing the dross receives the designation "tested and approved as genuine (δοκιμάζω)." Many present-day believers would argue, "God doesn't judge my love by the amount of money I give." But Paul and, if you believe the 2 Corinthians is inspired, the Holy Spirit do indeed, at times, test the pureness of a person's love with the measure of finances.

9. For you know about the graciousness of our Lord Jesus Christ. Although he was rich, yet for the benefit of you, he became poor, so that by means of his poverty you might become wealthy.

Paul uses the ultimate example of giving embodied in the life of Christ. In Philippians 2:5, he says "Let the attitude exemplified in Christ Jesus be in you." Now Paul exhorts the church to "let the same level of giving lived out in Jesus Christ flow into [their] financial life."

Jesus sat on His throne in a trouble-free realm brimming with infinite goodness as millions of angels and redeemed souls perpetually worshiped Him. The Lord of Glory willingly stepped off the throne, slipped into an embryonic body, and exited the womb into a world swimming in sin and death. He then subjected Himself to imperfect parents and angry mobs, endured every unthinkable temptation, wore a crown of thorns with his entire back fileted open, carried a cross comprised of a tree he spoke into existence, and then drank to very bottom the cup filled with God's furious anger.

This unspeakable gift makes all who believe unspeakably rich for all eternity. In light of such a pacific sacrifice, how can the gift's recipients not part with a bit of money?

Much debate has raged over whether or not the word "rich" (πλουτέω/*pluteo*) refers to material wealth or spiritual riches. Many contend that the passage does not speak of material blessings at this juncture. However, both the word's usual meaning and Paul's flow of thought point to material wealth. πλουτέω refers more often than not to material riches. Also, the entire context of the passage points to the use of financial resources in advancing the kingdom. Nevertheless, even if Paul does employ πλουτέω to shine the light on spiritual blessings, that in no way downplays material prosperity. The Father's character never allows for giving the greater (spiritual wealth) while withholding the lesser (material wealth). Indeed, "Since he did not spare even his own Son but gave him up for us all, won't he also give us everything else?" (Rom. 8:32 NLT).

The verb πλουτήσητε (*pluteo*) stands in the aorist, subjunctive, active construction. The aorist tense speaks of a summary, completed action in the past. This means that Jesus both becoming poor and making the believer wealthy has already, concerning His part, taken place. The subjunctive mood signifies a high probability, but not certainty. As discussed in previous chapters of this commentary, the reason for the lack of certainty here concerns the free will of the subject. Believers must choose, by faith, to reach out and grab the benefits of this verse.

Finally, the active voice connotes the subject of doing the action of the verb. In this case, the believers stand as the subject. In summation, the latter part of this verse means His poverty gave you the opportunity to reach out with the hand of faith and grab hold of the wealth He already provided.

Of course, one must not overlook the context of this verse. The stingy believer holding what he falsely believes to be his money cannot possibly lay hold of the financial blessings of God. Furthermore, Paul explains in verse 5 that the Macedonians gave "themselves to the Lord." The principles of giving and receiving God's way work neither as mechanistic formulas nor spiritual good luck charms. James makes it clear that those seeking to apply this truth from a self-centered aim only waste their time. Even if they receive the blessings, they would δαπανήσητε *(dapanao), or* "'squander' it upon their own selfish aims" (James 4:3).

The miracle of receiving only flourishes in the lives of those embodying the grace of giving. The grace of giving only lives through those who first give themselves fully over to the will of the Father. God has no interest in funding the desires of the covetous, no matter how many times they use His name. However, God moves heaven and earth to funnel financial resources to those fully given over to advancing His kingdom.

8:10–15

10. Here is my advice [opinion] concerning this matter: It will benefit you to finish what you began doing. Last year you were the first to not only desire to get the giving campaign started, but you actually began doing it. 11. Now you must complete what you started. Let the willingness to do it that you demonstrated, carry over into actually doing it. Give in proportion to what you have. 12. If the willingness to give is there, give according to what you have and not what you don't have.

A year before Paul writes 2 Corinthians, the church spoke with great vigor about sowing into the offering for Jerusalem. However, as so often happens, the heat of generosity had cooled to a nearly frozen frugality. Improper responses to conflict afford Satan the opportunity to infuse doubt regarding leadership competency. This can be seen as far back as the troubling issues between Moses and the Israelites. Then, discontentment with "the way things are going" leads to a weakened faithfulness in giving. Paul challenges them to finish what they started. The Corinthians need not give more than they have. If they have overpromised, Paul only asks them to do what they can.

13. I do not mean that your giving should take the responsibility off of others and make it difficult for yourselves.

The church in Corinth needs to begin doing their part to relieve a portion of the load borne by other churches. When one leg refuses to function as designed, the other leg carries an abnormally high proportion of the work.

14. There should be equality. At this time, your abundance can supply for the challenge of their current situation. Later, when they have abundance, they can supply when your finances face a challenge. This creates balance. 15. As it is written "He who gathered plenty had nothing left over; and he who gathered little had no lack."

Like every other task Christ empowers and commissions his body with, giving financially works best when "each part does its own special work." This unification "helps the other parts grow, so that the whole body is healthy and growing and full of love" (Eph. 4:16 NLT). This truth comes encapsulated in the word ἰσότης (isotes) often translated into English as "equality." Greek uses this term to signify "equality of parts working cooperatively within a whole." In order for the whole to function at designed capacity, its parts must both fit accurately and move together in unison.[2]

The word σχίσμα (schisma) means "division'" "split,'" or "tear," and stands as an antonym for ἰσότης. Indeed, "no one puts a piece of unshrunk cloth on an old garment; for the patch pulls away from the garment, and the tear (σχίσμα) is made worse" (Matt. 9:16 NKJ).

A church operating in financial unity possesses unique potential to advance the kingdom of heaven and destroy the works of the devil. Conversely, a body of believers split apart regarding monetary issues unwittingly beckons to the enemy, "Come tear us apart."

The Holy Spirit graciously floods hearts with this otherworldly equality. Believers channeling the river outward will, in time, see its effects in financial generosity. Others allow a mere trickle of outflow by damming the river with branches comprised of unrenewed patterns of thought. Those truly moved with compassion step into the God kind of generosity. When presented with the needs of others, they refuse to deceptively cloak financial apathy in the garb of "I'll pray for you."

8:16–24

16. Thank God! He has given Titus the same zealous care for you that I have.

Paul plans on sending Titus and two other unnamed believers to Corinth for the purpose of taking up their special offering.

17. For Titus not only accepted our request, but he himself was very excited to go see you.

He explains that Titus exhibited preexisting excitement to visit the church. Like those contributing, the one taking up the offering does so with cheerfulness.

18. We sent another brother along with Titus. All the church praise him as a preacher of the gospel. 19. Furthermore, he was chosen by the churches to travel with us regarding this financial gift, which we administer in order to glorify the Lord, and show our eagerness to help. 20. This precaution will guard against any discrediting us in our oversight of this generous [large] gift.

Paul praises the rightness of having three people taking up and transporting the offering. This protocol safeguards against either real or imagined financial scandal. The screen of church history is littered with examples of financial mismanagement. Following Paul's example here would greatly curb the massive tide of financial improprieties so prevalent in today's church world. For Paul, credibility in this role rests not with spiritual gifting alone, but with a proven track record of godly character. Without question, Titus bears the stamp of Paul's approval. Furthermore, the Corinthians had previous personal interaction with Titus. However, in addition to one from his own camp,

Paul sends a representative from the church in Jerusalem. Thus, a liaison from both the collectors and benefactors of the offering play a part in the entire process. Concerning finances, rampant covertness often fosters rabid corruption. Covertness and covetousness often live as symbiotic twins. Paul did not say, "We are all believers. God sees our hearts; let's just trust one another."

21. For we exercise great care to do what is honorable not only in the eyes of the Lord, but also in the eyes of people. 22. In addition, we are sending another brother who has proven himself sincere in many times in many different situations. He is now even more eager to help because of his great confidence in you. 23. If anyone asks about Titus, he is my partner [in all my endeavors] and helper concerning you [the ministry in Corinth]. The brothers traveling with him are reprentatives of the churches and they bring glory to Christ. 24. Therefore show to them, both in private and before the church, the genuineness of your love and of our boasting on your behalf.

The phrase "to do what is honorable" in verse 21 comes from the Greek word προνοέω (pronoeo). This term means "to make careful consideration in advance." Thus, προνοέω connotes the idea of "carefully conducting oneself with honor in a matter." Regarding this offering, Paul argues for such honorable dealings in both the sight of God and man. Some fearfully view financial accountability as a mechanism of control. Rather than increasing manipulation, proper accountability increases the free flow of funds.

When Moses oversaw the building of the tabernacle, he gave a detailed accounting of the finances. In no way did this accounting alter the plans God gave. Regardless of what others thought, the tabernacle was built according to God's design and not the whims of its financiers. Likewise, the offering for the Jerusalem church would be allocated according to the direction God gave Paul. Nevertheless, he ensured that three exceptionally trustworthy people would "travel together to stand above any talk of scandal regarding the handling of this extravagant gift."

9:1–15 Overflowing Abundance

9:1–5

1. Now concerning the offering for the saints in Jerusalem; I don't really even need to write you about it.

In many ways, chapter 9 mirrors Paul's flow of thought already dispersed in the previous chapter. For example, he once again produces the sound of sarcasm by plucking the heartstrings comprised of the boisterous Macedonia-Achaia rivalry. This chord of sarcasm comes through loud and clear in the statement "Concerning the offering for the saints in Jerusalem; I do not really even need to write you about it." In this statement, Paul brilliantly uses the adjective form περισσόν (perissos) of the verb περισσεύω (perissuo) meaning "more than enough" or "over the top" used in 8:6. In other words, "It is really over the top that I even need to write you again about it."

Paul holds the church at Corinth accountable to their year-old promise of financial support for the saints in Jerusalem. The Corinthians' initial foundation of intended generosity had begun to break down under the hammers of everyday life. Pledges put off until tomorrow had advanced to next week, which quickly gave way to next year. Making financial promises for "someday" often creates nothing more than a place wherein misguided intentions lay the empty eggs of "I meant to." Wisdom dictates that monetary pledges have an accompanying, specified end date.

Other expenses took precedence over the gift the Corinthians had previously promised. Now they must move toward completing their promise by doing their best now. Therefore, in these few verses, Paul uses several words meaning to "prepare" or "make ready."

From Genesis through Revelation, the principle of preparedness in giving, rather than afterthought, jumps from nearly every page of Scripture. Thousands of years before the Law of Moses, Abel carefully prepared an animal sacrifice while Cain haphazardly brought some of his produce. Throughout ancient Israel, not a single citizen dared enjoy the fruit of the earth until a designated representative crossed the temple threshold with the firstfruits. Today, those intending to give financially after paying all the bills often end up owing God. The practice of setting aside tithes and offerings before accounting for other obligations places both the believer and God in a much better position. This arrangement gives the believer an opportunity to exercise faith, and, as a result, God has the opportunity to fulfill His Word.

2. I know how willing you are to help, and I have been boasting about you to the Macedonians, telling them that you in Achaia have been ready [to send an offering] since last year. [Hearing of] your excitement has stirred most of them to action.

He loads up verse 2 with a series of perfect tense verbs to signify completed action with ongoing effects in the present and future. This grammatical construction, along with Paul's word choice, sends a strong message of accountability. He explains that "I have prior personal knowledge of οἶδα (oida), your eager willingness to give. Based on this, I am currently bragging (καυχῶμαι/kauchaomai) to the Macedonians that you in Achaia have already had everything prepared (παρεσκεύασται/paraskeuazo) as far back as one year ago." This reveals that what one promises at a specified point in time has ongoing effects. In the realm of promises, neutrality does not exist. A promise made either manifests into faithfulness in the form of a promise fulfilled or faithlessness in a promise abandoned.

3. Yet I have sent the brothers to ensure that our boasting on you may not prove empty concerning the matter of you being ready to give.

God pays out on his promises without fail. Thus, the believer's boasting in Him is never in vain. In this area, God's children ought to imitate their Father.

4. For if any of the Macedonians come with me and find you not ready, we — and certainly you as well — would be ashamed of having such confidence in you.

Paul exhorts the Corinthians to avoid the embarrassment of standing unprepared regarding their offering. Corinth's fervor first sparked generosity in the Macedonian church. A lack of readiness in Corinth will cause their example to move from something admirable slated for imitation to a thing shameful marked for avoidance.

5. Therefore, I deemed it necessary to urge the brothers to visit you beforehand and ensure that the gift you already promised is ready. It should be ready as an abundantly generous gift and not one given grudgingly [with regret attached to it].

Instead, they should fulfill the "promise they have already made." This phrase comes from the Greek verb προεπηγγελμένην (*prokatagg-ello*) standing in the perfect tense. The same term, also, in the perfect tense applies to the "gospel promised beforehand in the Holy Scriptures" (Rom. 1:1–2). The gospel carries with it a fulfillment of promise. This fits with Paul's challenge that the Corinthians "fulfill," "complete," or "finish" their promised pledge.

Jesus stands as the "author and finisher (τελειωτήν/*teleiotes*) of your faith" (Heb. 12:2). Without question, "He who began working in you will see things through to completion (ἐπιτελέσει/*epiteleo*)" (Phil. 1:6). In light of God's faithfulness in completing his promises, Paul challenges the Corinthians to fulfill their promise. Earlier, in chapter 8 verse 11, he uses the imperative verb form ἐπιτελέσατε (*epiteleo*), meaning "I command you to fulfill your promise of giving."

The word translated as "grudgingly" or "with covetousness" comes from the Greek term πλεονεξ (*pleonexia*) meaning "an unquenchable desire for more possessions." This compound word forms by attaching the adjective, πλέον (*pleon*) meaning "a large amount of possessions" with the noun ἐξουσία (*exousia*) meaning "authority in a decision-making capacity."[11] Taken together, the word more accurately means "one exercising authority regarding the allocation of possessions."

The idea that an offering is a choice to allocate a portion of one's possessions to God remains a lie. Humans both enter and exit the temporal realm without a single possession. Any possessions one has never truly stand under that person's jurisdiction. The individual only stands in the position of steward and never owner. The word πλεονεξί may also result from an alloying of πλέον (pleon) with ἔχω (echo) meaning "to hold tightly to." In this case, πλεονεξί means "to be tightfisted regarding abundance."

The deception of πλεονεξί comes from a clouded heart. The one viewing possessions as things to be owned and thereby controlled has stepped into a demonic trap. Jesus cried out "Beware! Guard against every kind of greed. Life is not measured by how much you own" (Luke 12:15 NLT). The heart caught in such deception cannot have true financial abundance. In truth, no matter how large their bank account, possessions have them instead of them having possessions.

However, those viewing money as a tool for advancing the kingdom can experience massive abundance in every area of life including finances. Because God's word exposes the lie of materialism does not mean it simultaneously veils prosperity. If having abundance automatically and necessarily leads to corruption, then God must be corrupt. The Lord possesses wealth beyond measure while, at the same time, never exhibiting a hint of impurity. If believers should walk as representatives of God's character, why should they not also mirror His provision?

9:6–15

6. [Never forget] this: the one planting a measly amount will also harvest a measly crop. But the one planting lavishly will harvest a bountiful crop.

The word translated as "measly" comes from the Greek term φειδομένως (pheidomenos) meaning "a small, limited amount." Writers most often assign the verb forms of this word to display something important held back for oneself. When speaking of the Father's love for His children, Paul exclaims that "God did not hold back (ἐφείσατο/ pheidomai) the Son uniquely belonging to Himself, but handed Him over to the betrayers for us" (Rom. 8:32). The totality of God's riches remained wrapped up in the package of Jesus. Paul bookends this thought by praising God for his "far too great for words gift!" Surely the recipients of the incalculable gift of Christ have no legitimacy for measuring out things to hold back. Instead, believers have the grand opportunity to plant with abundance and thereby reap an exceptionally heavy harvest.

The term translated "lavishly" comes from the Greek word εὐλογία (eulogia) also meaning "blessing." Paul and early Christians called the communion cup, "the cup of εὐλογία (blessing)."[2] Abundance springing from a heart of love always produces blessing. Jesus gave, not a drop, but every drop of His blood.

7. Each one of you should decide in his own heart; not grudgingly or under painful pressure; for God loves a cheerful giver.

Paul then lays out the proper motivation for giving. People should give as they have προῄρηται (proaireo): "made careful determination in their own hearts." Here, "the heart" refers to one's spirit or innermost being. This works in concert with Paul's caution against giving motived by the manipulative power of guilt.

The phrase "painful pressure" comes mainly from the Greek term ἀνάγκη (anagke) meaning "pressure from dire circumstances" or "pressure to fulfill a duty." When people find themselves in trouble, they become vulnerable to guilt-ridden, fund-raising tactics. This pressure tugs on both the mental and emotional components of the soul.

Despair filled thoughts such as "I better do this or I will be in trouble" ignite fretful emotions rooted in fear. A begrudging, negatively charged soul never serves as a seedbed for sprouting faith. The one giving from a confident spirit, radiates a positive excitement that God loves. Uncommon cheerfulness or "hilarity" proves the proper response from those believing in the irrefutable law of planting and harvesting.

8. And God is able to make all grace abound in your favor, so that you have all sufficiency in all things at all times, having all that you need to produce in you more than enough for every good work.

No one can claim they have nothing to give. Paul assigns two powerful Greek words to drive home this point. The term περισσεύω, meaning "a more than enough, overflowing abundance" again makes an appearance. Paul also uses the short, albeit immensely far reaching, word πᾶς (pas), translated "all" five times in a single sentence. At one point, he lines up the word three consecutive times to demonstrate how God's grace empowers "you in *all* things at *all* times (παντὶ πάντοτε πᾶσαν/pas pantote pas), having *all* that you need to produce in you more than enough for every good work."

Here, Paul uses the subjunctive, present, active verb construction περισσεύητε for "more than enough" while ἔχοντες (echo) stands in the present active participle form "having." This means that the "all sufficiency" they currently possess remains potentially available for more than enough for the accomplishment of every good work. The "good works" spoken of here pertain to blessing others via giving financially. Lack never results from a real absence of resources, but instead from the unwise distribution of what God disperses. The blessings of God already made available in Christ do not automatically manifest on earth. Faith grabs hold of the "all sufficiency" and makes it work with a "more than enough abundance" in the course of blessing others.

James speaks exactly to this point by highlighting the role of faith in receiving God's promises. Nevertheless, this faith must be exercised in the course of fulfilling the kingdom of God and not for merely for one's "own selfish consumption" (James 4:3).

Some mistakenly look disparagingly on "wealthy preachers." Certainly, some ministers amass fortunes through mastering manipulative offering techniques. Others, however, have voraciously sought first the kingdom and its righteousness and thereby had "all these [material] things added to them."

The Greek word δικαιοσύνη (dikaiosune), in addition to meaning "right standing with God (rightouesness)," can also mean "doing the right thing under God's guidance." In other words, the same grace that has made believers righteous also empowers them to behave rightly. John highlights this by saying, "If you know that He is righteous, you know that everyone who practices righteousness is born of Him" (1 John 2:29 NKJ).

9. As it is written: "He has spread his resources widely to the poor; his righteousness remains forever.

Paul states that the one giving to those in need has a "righteousness that will be remembered into eternity." Those helped through the generosity of others will remember that righteous act forever. Joyous givers cannot help but be blessed with abundance! Whenever resources come into their hands, they give them away at the direction of the Spirit. Then, true to His Word, the Lord entrusts them with even more. Solomon noted this with the pithy proverb: "He who has pity on the poor lends to the Lord, And He will pay back what he has given" (Prov. 19:17 NKJ).

Those misunderstanding abundance tend to view God as having a limited supply. If God only has so much to go around, it can seem selfish for some to have lots while others have little. If, however, God has an unlimited supply, He can make "all grace abound" to as many as He can trust. The Lord has never said to anyone, "I would love to help, but I'm a little short this month myself." The all sufficient one scours the earth for those He can flow through financially. There are no "pieces of the pie" to fight over, only people to serve.

10. Now, may the one supplying seed to the planter and bread for food supply and multiply your seed planted and increase your harvest of righteousness. 11. You will be enriched in everything so that you can be generous. This causes thanksgiving through us to God. 12. For this ministry of service is not only supplying for the needs of the saints, but is also overflowing as many offer thanksgiving to God.

In verse 10, God promises seed for the "planter" (σπείρω/*speiro*). The construction here is a present, active participle meaning "the one presently engaged in the activity of planting." Those saying, "Once God really blesses me financially, I will become a big giver" have deceived themselves. Although the Lord has unlimited resources, He never uses them unwisely. God will not give seed to those thinking, wishing, or dreaming of sowing. This seed, when planted and watered turns into a harvest from which people can eat bread. God will not only "give" seed to active planters, He will also "multiply" (πληθύνω/*plethuno*) it.

Paul also uses the future tense πληθυνεῖ to speak of something guaranteed to happen in the future. Additionally, the verb for "greatly increase" (αὐξήσει/*auxano*) stands in the future tense. This same word came from the mouth of Jesus when speaking the parable of the planter.

According to the Master, the seed in the good ground "multiplied abundantly." The future tense verbs, πληθυνεῖ and αὐξήσει, announce the guarantee that those planting in productive soil will receive a divine multiplication of seed resulting in a greatly enlarged harvest. Conversely, true riches will always elude those giving either from mere obligation or messy manipulation.

Those living generously also have the added blessing of serving as instruments of thanksgiving to God. Although all the glory goes to the Lord, He actually funnels the thanksgiving "through us" to Himself. Thus the grace of giving allows for the fulfillment of "his will being done on earth as it is heaven" as "He gives us our daily bread" and results in His "being the kingdom and the power and the glory forever."

13. They will give glory to God because of your ministry expressed in confession of the gospel of Christ with accompanying obedience, and for the generous contribution to them and all people [you minister to]. 14. And they will pray for you with relentless desire because of the overflowing grace of God in you. 15. Thank God for His gift, far too wonderful for words!

In verse 13, Paul states that truly effective ministry is "expressed in confession of the gospel of Christ with accompanying obedience." Teaching, no matter how balanced, thorough, and rooted in Scripture, must progress into action. Frequent and accurate teaching remains a must for anyone serious about maturing in the Lord. Without faith, it is impossible to excel in the Christian life. Faith comes by hearing the Word preached. However, many believers jump, week after week for years, on the spiritual treadmill constructed of hearing, but never doing. Ever learning, but never really possessing the degree of knowledge only had by means of experience.

The body of Christ would do well to follow the example of its head who both "taught and did" (Acts 1:1). The Good Samaritan preached, with his actions, one of the greatest sermons ever proclaimed. Mark speaks of the Holy Spirit "confirming the Word with corresponding action expressed in miraculous signs and wonders" (Mark 16:20). In order for the Spirit to act in confirming the Word, believers must first act upon what the Word states. How fitting that the very book detailing the earliest church bears the name "Acts." People "will give glory to God because of your ministry" when they see love "demonstrating the truth by acting upon it" (1 John 3:18).

10:1–18 A Humble Mind

10:1–6

1. Now I, Paul, implore you with the meekness and gentleness of Christ — [as some of you say] I am too timid toward you when in person, but bold when away.

Chapter 10 opens with a stream that grows into a raging river by the time it reaches chapter 12. This Spirit-inspired waterway consists of a startling contrast between worldly posturing for glory and true, Christlike greatness.

Paul's opponents have carefully constructed a platform from this world's measuring sticks for success. While speaking with a strange alloy of acerbic sarcasm and genuine meekness, he smashes their stage with a sledgehammer truth. Paul's enemies have labeled him as a two faced leader. They portray him as a pushover while in Corinth and a tyrant in his letters.

Paul nearly begs them to see these charges as patently absurd. He explains that if they do not believe him in the letter, they will surely believe it when he arrives. Paul has no reservations about standing toe to toe with these spiritual bullies.

The "meekness" (πραΰτης/praotes) with which he reaches out does carry with it an inherent shrinking from conflict. πραΰτης expresses "consideration of others to the point of yielding." The meek do not always seek to get their share first and foremost. They consistently consider others above themselves. The meek trust the Lord to take care of them while they seek to care for others.

However, meekness does not stand idly by while the enemy uses people to hinder God's kingdom. Scripture portrays Moses, the "meekest man on the earth" (πραΰς in the Septuagint) smashing the tablets of the Law, grinding an idol to powder, mixing that nasty substance with water, and forcing the Israelites to drink it down. He had no hesitation to, at times, take swift and decisive action against the enemies of God.

2. I beg you that, when I come, I will not have to be as bold as I plan to be toward some who think of us as having carnal motives.

Paul expresses more than a mere possibility of confronting his opponents. The verb λογίζομαι (*logizomai*) meaning "to carefully measure out" stands in the present middle indicative construct. Thus, Paul is in the middle of mulling over a precise plan of attack for his next visit.

3. Although we live in mortal bodies, we do not develop and carry out battle plans in the way humans do.

This assault will not come with fists and feet. Although he "currently lives in a body," Paul neither develops nor executes battle plans according to the flesh. The phrase "battle plans" comes from the Greek term στρατεύομαι (*strateuomai*) meaning "carrying out diligently crafted military orders." Greek writers assigned the word to those in active military service. Those throughout the Greco-Roman world would have certainly identified with the term στρατεύομαι. The culture of Rome ruling the day rested, above all else, in its military prowess. Unlike Greece, soldiers, far more than philosophers, comprised the luminaries brightening Rome's cultural sky. In particular, the inhabitants of Corinth personally held στρατεύομαι not as an auxiliary and fanciful concept, but rather as a cardinal issue of life and death.

The Corinthians knew full well that military strategy both shook its history to its core and shaped its present. Over 500 years before the gospel first walked into the city, the famous General Adeimantus of Corinth served as a commander during the Persian invasion under King Xerxes. Furthermore, around 380 BC, Philip II, King of Macedon and father of the world's greatest military strategist of all time (Alexander the Great), also left a lasting impression on the

Corinthian saga. After exercising a triumph-producing strategy at the battle in Chaeronea, Phillip united the city-states of Greece into a single force designed to rebuff relentless Persian interference. This coalition bears the name of its initial gathering: "The League of Corinth."

In the era of the Republic, general Lucius Mummius set out to bring all of Greece under Roman control. In 146 BC, all Corinthian attempts at στρατεύομαι failed as Mummius overthrew Corinth's soldiers, killed its men, took its women and children into slavery, looted its treasuries, and burned the city to the ground. The Corinthians had a wide landing strip for all the militaristic terms, including στρατεύομαι, dropped on them by Paul. In modern times, it would be akin to using computing terms when communicating with those based in Silicon Valley during America's high tech boom.

The preposition κατά (kata) in the genitive case can mean both "by means of" and "against." Paul uses it to say both, "we do not war by means of the flesh" and "we do not pit flesh against flesh."

4. The weapons we use for warfare are not worldly, but mighty in God for the purpose of demolishing of strongholds.

God has armed believers with powerful ὅπλον (hoplon) "weapons." Greeks applied this word as a title for heroic citizen-soldiers armed with long spears and shields. The Captain of the Lord's hosts has called believers, as citizens of heaven, into active military service. These weapons are not associated with the fallen, earthly realm (σαρκικός/sarkikos), but "mighty" through God. Worldly leaders, at every level, seek to rise higher by means of pulling others down. Soldiers of the cross seek to lift others higher even at their own expense.

Not a single weapon of God is designed to lift up His army by debasing other people. The Lord never funds, energizes, or even gives the nod to ego inflating activities. The church possesses weapons for pulling down prideful demonic positions in order to lift up hurting humanity.

The word translated "mighty" here comes from the Greek term δυνατός (dunatos) meaning "strong" or "immensely powerful." However, this word can also mean "possible." The Lord gives every soldier weapons against which the enemy's attacks cannot possibly stand. God has thought of every possible scenario hell might plan. In His infinite wisdom, the Lord has blessed the church with weapons πρός (*pros* [in the accusative case]) — meaning 'for the purpose of' — assaulting, dismantling, and decimating the place where once stood demonic ὀχύρωμα (*ochuroma*), or 'stoutly built fortresses.' "

5. We are dismantling false reasoning and every high place raised up in opposition to the knowledge of God. We capture these ungodly thoughts and bring them into obedience to Christ, 6. maintaining a state of readiness to behave justly regarding all disobedience once your obedience is lived out.

Many think of strongholds consisting of seemingly unshakable, destructive addictions. Satan strategizes in a much more cleaver manner. He knows that wrong thinking automatically produces wrong behavior. Lies serve as the building blocks of every stronghold. In the garden, the serpent did not start with "beat your wife, manufacture an idol, and begin worshipping it." One lie, lodged in the mind, left unchecked against the Word opened the door more than wide enough. The stronghold of "you will not die if you eat; you will be like God" unleashed an incalculable number of wicked actions into Adam's descendants.

In Ephesians 6, Paul catalogues the hierarchy of demonic forces (Eph. 6:12). True to form, Satan copied the chain of command the Lord created for his angels (Col. 1:16). The "rulers of the darkness of this world" comprise one of the top levels for evil spirits. These unclean spirits plan strategies for advancing the kingdom of darkness in the earth. They know that wrong thinking produces twisted value systems and twisted value systems bear the fruit of evil behaviors. These spirits seize hold of various platforms for dispensing their dark philosophies. Some of their favorite platforms include the entertainment industry, universities, and, sadly at times, churches. In large part, it's a matter of demonic economics: the larger the audience, the more valuable to the devil's workers.

Again, the "strongholds" are built, not from bad behavior, but un-godly value systems. The entertainment industry peddles the lie that women serve as nothing more than sexual objects. This, in turn fuels behaviors such as addiction to pornography. Universities teach that humans originated from chance collisions of nonsentient matter. This makes way for a value system lacking destiny. If humanity arrived on the scene without purpose, we must exit the stage, not into an eternal heaven or hell, but into nothingness. Politicians put forth the philos-ophy that life begins at some arbitrary point instead of conception. This produces the belief that unborn babies bear some kind of stand-ing below a full human being. This manner of thinking has, to Satan's delight, splashed massive buckets of blood onto the canvas of history.

If a church believes the false philosophy that certain parts of Scrip-ture are inspired and others lack inspiration, certain destruction will follow. Strongholds involving false beliefs concerning God's Word prove the strongest variety of all. When a person chooses to give lies a place of prominence in their mind, those lies can take root in the heart. The false reasoning (λογισμός/logismos) expounded on here re-sults, not so much from unintentional ignorance, but open rebellion. These prideful thoughts ἐπαιρόμενον/epairo are lifting themselves up in opposition to the knowledge of God.

When writing to Timothy, Paul urges Timothy to wield the weap-on of truth to those encased in strongholds to "come to their senses and escape from the devil's trap. For they have been held captive by him" (2 Tim. 2:25–26 NLT). The "capturing" of deceptive thoughts makes way for the freeing of the bewitched. Capturing such thoughts allows one to view them juxtaposed with the truth, against which they appear truly hideous. Paul calls these deceptive thoughts ὕψωμα (hupsoma), or "(high) things," that ἐπαιρόμενον (epairo), "lift them-selves up."

In the natural, any wise military strategist builds the city's strong-hold on very high ground. In Corinth, the city's highest point, com-prised of a massive rock formation is known as the Acrocorinth (seen on the cover of this commentary). Generals wisely built a massive, nearly impenetrable fortress on this very site. Several times throughout history, soldiers defended the region from invaders by utilizing this sturdy fortress.

In addition to Corinth, the building of cities on high places remained a penchant of Hellenistic city planners throughout Greek expansion. Although this architectural obsession became most glaring during Alexander's time and shortly thereafter, its roots go down below the strata of the Classical period and into the Mycenaean era. Here, among the ruins, archaeologists have uncovered high places whereupon lie the remains of fortresses. Not just any high level area of rock proved a suitable place for constructing a fortress. The building of a stronghold required two things: a water source and fertile ground. Once a location met such criteria, city walls and other defenses went up around well-watered, fertile high places. In similar fashion, demonic strongholds require both a stream of lies and fertile ground for deception.

In the Classical period, the Parthenon, Erechtheion, and temple of Athena Nike proudly perched on the Acropolis in Athens all served as testimonies of supposedly "high and lifted up" deities. It is no coincidence that the twelve great gods of Greece's pantheon reside nearly 3,000 feet up on Mount Olympus.

When an army mounted a successful attack on a city's perimeter, that city's forces would flee into the walls of its stronghold. There, they would regroup in order to launch a counterattack. When God begins to break down deception in a person, demonic force often refuse to immediately surrender. Instead, they restrategize for the purpose of a counter strike, into the stronghold of the mind.

When writing to the Ephesians, Paul commands them to "give no territory to the devil." This happens first at the entry points of one's life. The word translated "territory" comes from the Greek term τόπος (topos) meaning "a distinct region or area." Writers also use it to denote "a seaport" (cf. Acts 27:2). The enemy first assails believers at the entry ports of their eyes, ears, and mouths before entrenching in their minds. Once on the land of the soul, Satan begins seeking out mental "high places" as locales for πλεονεκτέω (pleonekteo) "deceptively exploiting" his victims by means of νόημα (noema), or "reasoning schemes" (2 Cor. 2:11). πλεονεκτέω is a compound word comprised of the Greek terms πλειῶν (pleion) and ἔχω (echo). The adjective πλειῶν signifies "a great degree of something" and translates to "much" or "many." The oft used verb ἔχω connotes the concept of "to have, hold tightly to, or forcefully grab for something." Therefore, πλεονεκτέω means "to seek claim to more than one is rightfully due." It also finds frequent usage to describe a "greedy" person. The devil relentlessly seeks to take more than he already possess. His greed for territory respects no boundary and possesses no stop button.

Interestingly, Paul places πλεονεκτέω in the passive verb form πλεονεκτηθῶμεν. The enemy can only take unauthorized ground from believers bowing to his pressure and allowing him to take it. Cowering down and accepting the "victim" label makes way for Satan's greedy grasping. Believers possessing a revelation of their position in Christ can reject the victim label for the banner of victor. Paul stands as a living example that no matter how tough things get, Christians can always take ground and never lose it.

The obsession with high places signifying the power of an empire's military, economy, and deities carried over from Greece to Rome. Indeed, twin demigods founded the nation upon a series of tall hills. The very name Ῥώμη (Rhome), meaning "strength," displays itself in the final four letters of ὀχύρωμα.

The theme of constructing "high places" remains woven into both the character and history of Satan. Shorty after the flood, he inspired Nimrod to construct an immense, high tower later called Babel. Later, he spurred rouge priests to set up "high places" where initiates would worship idols. Even the Acrocorinth, had, at its highest point, an altar to the false goddess Aphrodite. This fact corresponds well with both the theology of chapter 10 and the cultural malaise greatly corrupting the church at Corinth. Aphrodite (Venus) displays a feverish, out of control sexual obsession. In nearly every context, she appears totally nude. Aphrodite shows no hesitation in proving regularly unfaithful to her husband Hephaestus.

As stated before, deceitful thoughts give birth to twisted beliefs, and such beliefs result in dastardly behaviors. The temple of Aphrodite housed a financially prosperous and morally bankrupt prostitution enterprise. Sea captains from every sector of the Empire spun sordid tales of escapades in Corinth with exploited "female companions" (ἑταίρα/hetaira). Paul's repeated admonitions against a putrid parade of sexual dysfunctions in Corinth reveal the beast of sexual perversion, so pervasive in Corinthian society, beginning to lock down a chokehold upon the throat of the church.

Interestingly, the lust-immersed, self-admiring gorgon Medusa shares a close connection to Venus (Aphrodite). It comes as no surprise that a bevy of vipers nest upon Medusa's head (thought life). None of this should come as a surprise when coming from the one who, during his rebellion, cavalierly proclaimed, "I will set my throne above the stars of God!" (Isa. 14:13).

The believer possesses weapons designed by God for "pulling down" high thoughts by "capturing" (αἰχμαλωτίζοντες/aichmalotizo) them and forcing them to stand in the balance against the truth of God's Word. The light of truth then fully exposes all lies no matter how well camouflaged. This enables one to "stop conforming to this world's false value system and be transformed through getting the mind to think right" (Rom. 12:2). The fog of confusion, especially regarding the will of God, moves out and clarity sets in.

In other words, "Then you will be able to test and approve what God's will is — his good, pleasing and perfect will" (Rom. 12:2 NIV). In Romans, Paul describes a man engaged in a heated battle with "high thoughts." Although he "loves God's law with his innermost being (spirit), he recognizes another law in his body, warring against his mind, and capturing (αἰχμαλωτίζοντά) him to serve the law of sin" (Rom. 7:22–23). In this instance, as in all instances, the mind serves as the place where the battle rages. The enemy seeks to move past the mind and into the heart. He knows that "as a man thinks in his heart, so he becomes" (Prov. 23:7). Paul places both καθαιροῦντες (kathaireo), or "tearing down," and αἰχμαλωτίζοντες in the active verb voice. This means the believer must choose to unsheathe and use these exceedingly powerful weapons. Satan will not roll over and play dead out of pity. He, like all bullies, only responds to force.

10:7–12

7. You are judging merely by outward appearances. If anyone is sure within himself that he belongs to Christ, let him also

recognize [surely he can discern] that we belong to Christ as much as they do. 8. So even if I boast more about the authority the Lord has given us for building you up rather than tearing you down, I will not apologize for it. 9. I'm not attempting to terrify you with my letters.

Paul continues to contrast "building up" and "tearing down." In so doing, he amplifies the principle of God lifting up the humble and tearing down the proud. The Lord has given Paul authority, not to puff up his ego, but to serve the churches. The most effective preachers minister out of (and not as a substitute for) their relationship with God. Unlike his opponents, Paul does not relentlessly seek for security in man's approval. He already has it in Christ alone.

10. Some say, "The letters are pushy and forceful, but in person he is unimpressive, and his speeches are useless."

Some make a big stir about Paul's use of ἀσθενής (asthenes) in verse 10. Writers sometimes employ this word to signify "illness." Therefore the reasoning goes that Paul must have been so sickly that it made an impression on the Corinthians. However, the word Paul employs here does not work in concert with such a position. The Greek ἀσθενής comes from a merging of the word σθένος (sthenos), meaning physical strength, and the prefix a meaning "without." Thus, ἀσθενής often means "one without strength" or, as the *New American Standard Bible* renders it, "physically unimpressive." This was a way for Paul's enemies to say, "This guy is a wimp." He counters by appealing to Christ as his standard. More specifically, Paul cares not at all what they think of his outward appearance.

In His cross, the suffering savior displayed staggering strength through what appeared as appalling weakness. While Roman society ferociously stigmatized an apparent loser, all of heaven spotlighted the consummate winner.

11. Such people should consider that the way we are in our letters from afar will be seen in our actions when we arrive in person.

He meets the accusation concerning his alleged spineless behavior head on. Paul boldly tells them, "You will find out, when I arrive, that I can be just as forceful in person as you accuse me of being in my letters." While some may view this as overly confrontational, in no way does it run contrary to the character of Christ. Paul has neither the desire nor time to defend himself against anyone disliking him. He takes issue, however, with people seeking to undermine his authority within the church he overseers. One of the devil's favorite tactics is to stir up doubts in local churches regarding a leader's motives. Speaking behind the back of a leader often gets the job done with weak minded, self-absorbed, or very young believers. Against this cowardly trick, Paul responds, "If you don't like me, that's fine. However, if you have something to say about me to the sheep I pastor, say it to my face."

12. We dare not measure or compare ourselves with those obsessed with putting forth their own importance. When they compare themselves with each other by using each other as the standard of measurement, they are acting foolish.

He presents the process of people constantly measuring their success against arbitrary, man-made standards as utterly foolish. The word translated "measuring" comes from the Greek term μετρέω (*metreo*), meaning "take measurement" or "deal out and apportion." The English word "metric" also comes from this term.

Paul loves this term, μετρέω. In fact, he uses it four times in verses 12 and 13. In Romans, Paul warns that a man must not "think more highly of himself than he ought to think; but to think so as to have sound judgment, as God has allotted to each a measure (μέτρον/ *metrov*) of faith" (Rom. 12:3 NAS). Jesus had "the Spirit beyond measure (μέτρον)." God has given each person a special set of gifts as equipment for fulfilling a unique destiny. Exercising good stewardship of these giftings and thereby fulfilling one's destiny equals success. This can prove difficult for some.

At times, the church world fares not much better than the secular world concerning a propensity toward trendiness. When a certain style of worship is the all the rage, worship leaders often seek to copy gurus of the latest fad — all the way down to voice inflection and manner of dress. When the prophetic movement — bringing with it many good things and some bad — swept through the American church in the mid-nineties, "being prophetic" became a standard of measurement. Young preachers sometimes seek to parrot the mannerisms of their mentors. Many pastors carry around a hidden envy regarding other pastors with churches much larger than their own. All of these standards of measurement create a filthy pool Satan loves seeing God's children swim in.

A great freedom comes when one sees the standard of true success Paul sets forth to the Corinthians. The one constantly seeking conformity to earthy standards, including those bearing Christian labels, can never fully undergo transformation into the image of Christ. No one can serve both of these masters at the same time.

13. We will not boast beyond things done outside the sphere of our calling. We will only boast about what has happened within those boundaries; you certainly fall within those boundaries.

The desire for self-importance also manifests itself in stealing the work of another. Paul told the church in Rome, "It has always been my ambition to preach the gospel where Christ was not known, so that I would not be building on someone else's foundation." (Rom. 15:20 NIV). Erroneously claiming credit for the work of another amounts to a kind of identity theft growing out of the false measuring mentioned above.

14. We are not overreaching our boundaries by coming to you. For we were the first to come as far as you [Corinth] with the gospel of Christ, 15. not boasting of things outside our calling by claiming credit for the work of another. Instead, we hope that, as your faith grows, so will the scope of our work among you,

Ministers bent on name-dropping and sheep-stealing remain in a hellish trap no matter how large their empire grows. One can never fulfill their special, God-given task as long as they stay busy piggy-backing on the destiny of another.

16. to preach the gospel in areas beyond you [Corinth] and not to boast within the boundaries of someone else's work.

Paul contends that such ministers may have popularity, but they do not have authority. Accolades come from man, but true authority only comes from God to the humble. Godly authority does not manifest itself merely by ordering around a staff of yes men, but rather in signs, wonders, and selfless service. Paul seeks to expand his ministry, not on the coattails of another, but by empowering those he disciples to go make more disciples. He rounds out the chapter by asserting that real approval comes not from self-promotion, but from cooperating with the grace of God measured out as He wills.

17. Instead, "The one boasting should boast in the Lord." 18. When people commend themselves, it doesn't qualify them. True qualification comes from the Lord.

The world lauds and fawns over the self-absorbed. The belief that this metric has not infected the church serves as the epitome of credulity. Many lean on every word, whether accurate or not, falling from the mouths of popular preachers. These starstruck fans remain hypnotized by the glitz and glamour supporting a man-centered house of cards. God admires and empowers those seeking to remain unknown by the masses while making Christ known to all.

Of course, God sometimes gives exceptionally genuine ministers a worldwide audience. The Bible never speaks against a ministry or church for being large. If largeness equates to disingenuousness, God lives in such a state. He created a universe of nearly endless size.

11:1–33 Weak Boasting

11:1–12

1. Please bear with me while I play the fool. Indeed, you are bearing with me. 2. For I am jealous for you with a godly jealousy. I promised you as an unspoiled bride to only one husband: Christ.

In chapter 11, Paul dives head first into an activity he finds regrettably necessary: putting forth his own credentials. While often laughable, sometimes the arrogant posturing of spiritual bullies can endanger a flock. When this happens, even the meekest of God's servants must flex their gifting, calling, and character muscles in full view.

Although necessary, the humble never relish such times. Standing from a position of security in Christ, they have no point to prove. Paul does, however, have a flock to protect. Paul begins the chapter with the Greek word ὄφελονο (phelon). This particle serves to introduce indulgent requests. It can also speak of indebtedness. In other words, writers used it to say, "I will really owe you if you hear me out on this request."

Paul implores the Corinthians to bear with him as he "plays the fool." This word comes from the Greek term ἀφροσύνη (aphrosune) meaning "lacking proper thought." While the world praises boasting "in one's possessions and accomplishments" (1 John 2:16), Paul sees it as the realm for those not thinking right. Most, in one form or another, spend nearly all their time, talents, and treasure seeking a reputation of popularity. Jesus, while rightfully possessing the totality of prestige, willing "made himself of no reputation."

3. But I fear that your minds might be led astray from your devotion to Christ by the sneaky serpent just as he deceived Eve. 4. For if someone approaches you preaching a different Jesus than the one we preached, or if you receive a different spirit than the one you already received, or a gospel differ-

ing from the one you already accepted, you show no sign of protest. 5. You see, I don't consider myself inferior, in any manner, to these "super apostles."

Paul pulls no punches but lands a power shot by comparing his opponents directly to Satan. Similar to the serpent's beguiling of Eve, these "super apostles" strive to pull the church away from its founder and toward themselves. These enemies of the true gospel clearly hold up and embody "sophist" ideals of legitimacy.[1]

Other than the language of the New Testament, the voracious pursuit of wisdom remains Greece's greatest gift to humanity. Even the very term, "philosopher" memorializes this fact. The term comes from the compund of two Greek words: φιλέω (phileo), meaning "to love," and σοφία (sophia), or "wisdom." Hence, a philosopher is "one intensely loving wisdom."

6. I might be untrained as a speaker, but I know what I'm talking about [I have experienced it; it's not just rhetoric]. We made this perfectly clear to you in every way.

Around 400 BC, the philosophical star of Athens fell from its "golden" sky when the city-state of Sparta fully overran the city. This shocking defeat caused the disillusioned populace of Greece to drop its long held zeal for seeking absolute truth. A new breed of speaker arose roughly amounting to an ancient version of today's motivational gurus. These teachers of pop psychology developed public speaking into an art form known as "rhetoric."

In addition to Greek philosophy, the culture saw drastic changes in both its judicial and political arenas. Rather than impartial justice, lawyers most skilled in public speaking prevailed. The same phenomenon ruled the day in a political climate increasingly under the sway of democracy. A concern for objective truth became buried under carefully crafted and skillfully delivered speeches designed to maximize the moving of emotions.

Paul argues that this quagmire both has and will increasingly continue to infect believers intent on remaining self-absorbed. Just as deep calls to deep, shallow calls to shallow. A church full of carnal believers comfortably rocks itself to sleep when a man-pleasing preacher sits at its helm. In other words, a time is coming when people will no longer listen to sound and wholesome teaching. Instead, "they will follow their own desires and will look for teachers who will tell them whatever their itching ears want to hear" (2 Tim. 4:3 NLT). The sophists stood as rock stars of the ancient Greek world. They could demand exceptionally high fees for their services. Sophism fit into a cosmopolitan city such as Corinth like a hand in a glove.

Into such a fleshly, fad-centered setting steps Paul. These enemies quickly and repeatedly point out Paul's inferior speaking skills as evidence for the illegitimacy of his ministry. When one considers the enormity of Paul's education, it becomes obvious that he could have held his own in the sphere of public speaking. His lack of meticulously laying out every line of a speech stems, not from inferiority, but a desire to yield to the Holy Spirit. He notes this very thing in earlier correspondence with Corinth by saying, "Rather than using clever and persuasive speeches, I relied only on the power of the Holy Spirit" (1 Cor. 2:4 NLT).

In no way should one construe this to mean that Paul struggled with public speaking. Furthermore, Paul statement, "I stood before you in fear and much trembling" (1 Cor. 2:3) refers not to a lack of confidence in his speaking abilities, but shines forth a supreme awareness of his dependency on God. He knows full well that while natural talent may move the collective emotions of a crowd, only the Spirit can send demons packing, heal bodies, and transform lives.

However, Paul's proclivity toward experiencing the Spirit's power does not mean he either demeans or discards the need for both studying and dispersing sound doctrine. Preachers sometimes seek to use the Holy Spirit as a detour from rightly dividing the Word. They disguise their own exegetical laziness with spiritually sounding phrases such as, "I just rely on the Spirit to give me the words." In verse 6, Paul says, "Although I may not be the most skilled public speaker, I am not without knowledge."

7. Did I sin when I humbled myself in order to lift you up by preaching the gospel free of charge?

In addition to speaking disparagingly of Paul's speaking skills, his opponents maligned his lack of financial showmanship. While in Corinth, Paul did not receive any offerings for himself. His opponents seized on this as further proof of his inadequacy. The "greatest" speakers could demand cartloads of money for each speech. What kind of man must Paul be if he could never raise a single coin in a city as wealthy as Corinth? His opponents failed to realize that Paul's lack of offerings sprang from a refusal on his part and not the church's. So often, the world views love as weakness.

8. I even "robbed" other churches by receiving their offerings so I could serve you without charge. 9. When I was there [in Corinth] and needing anything, I never placed the financial burden on you. Instead, the brothers who came from Macedonia brought me what I needed. [Again] I refused to be a burden to you, and I never will be.

Paul once again brings up the concept of humility and arrogance by reminding the Corinthians that he lowered himself by not taking up offerings. He did this in order to lift them up and not put a financial strain on the church. Other churches financially subsidized his ministry in Corinth.

10. [Know that] as surely as the truth of Christ resides within me, no one in the entire regions of Achaia will stop me from boasting about this. 11. Why? Is it because I don't love you? God knows that I certainly do! 12. And I will keep on doing this in order to cut off the opportunity [to silence] from those who desire an opening to boast that they are [that they minster] just like us.

Not only does Paul not carry shame for this act of sacrifice, he doesn't mind if everyone in Greece finds out about it. The language here speaks of Paul's preference to have kept this whole matter a secret. He prefers the undercover method, not as a means of underhandedness, but in order to honor the church in Corinth.

11:13–20

13. These people are false apostles, deceitful workers who transform themselves into apostles truly sent from and belonging to Christ.

Paul yanks off his opponents' masks, grabs the attention of the Corinthians, and says, "Look at these imposters!" He does not call them "anti-apostles," but ψευδαπόστολοι (pseudapostolos), meaning "fake apostles." They may wear the clothes, speak the terms, and bear the title of apostles; However, this all proves an elaborate ruse.

The word often translated "transform" in verse 13 comes from the Greek term μετασχηματίζω (metaschematizo). When referring to thorough transformation, Paul uses the term μεταμορφόω (metamorphoo). μετασχηματίζω carries with it more a focus on outward appearance. For example, when speaking of the transformation of the believer's physical (outward) body, Paul uses μετασχηματίζω (Phil. 3:21).

When speaking of the transforming work of the Spirit in the New Covenant, Paul says "the Lord — who is the Spirit — makes us more and more like him as we are changed (μεταμορφόω)into his glorious image" (2 Cor. 3:18 NLT).

Thus, in verse 13, translating μετασχηματίζω as "disguise" proves more accurate. Here, Paul employs the present middle participle form of the verb μετασχηματιζόμενοι, meaning "those continuously cloaking themselves." Jesus also spoke of "those calling themselves apostles, but in reality they are not" (Rev. 2:2). The Old Testament also speaks of false prophets.

14. It certainly doesn't come as a shock! For even Satan masquerades himself as an angle of light.

In truth, Satan has crafted disguises for all of the fivefold ministry gifts listed in Ephesians 4:12. He constantly seeks to dress those with impure motives to slip into these costumes. Satan is the father of disguises. He wears the most intricate costume in the universe. Were men to see his true form, none but the most hardened would follow his call. This prince of darkness wraps himself in a mask composed of fake light.

Sadly, before his fall, God gave him the name Lucifer, meaning "the one bearing bright light." Conversely, the Lord "is the source and sum of light and in him is no darkness; not any at all" (1 John 1:5). Satan's costume may project fake light, but his works show forth real darkness.

15. Therefore, it is no big thing if his workers also masquerade as ministers of righteousness. [Rest assured,] their end will be commensurate with their works. 16. I repeat: Let no one take me for a fool. But even if you do, listen to me as you would a fool, so that I can boast for a short time. 17. When I speak like that, I am not speaking like the Lord would, but as a fool would in his boasting. 18. Since many have no hesitation to boast about themselves, I will also boast.

Satan's "light" is darkness, and the same holds true for both his demonic and human emissaries. For this reason, Paul tells the Corinthians not to be shocked at the masquerading tactics running wild in the church. Jesus said, "You will know people by their fruits," not by their titles. The title one claims reveals what one thinks of oneself. The fruit one bears manifests who one truly is.

19. Obviously, you have no problem indulging fools since you yourselves are so wise. 20. You tolerate it even if someone enslaves you, wipes out your resources, seeks to take even more, boasts about himself, and then slaps you in the face.

Paul exhorts the church to wise up and smell the deception. They view themselves as wise, yet they have allowed foolishness to cover them like a blanket.

11:21–23

21. To my shame, I must admit we were too weak for that. What anyone else would strive to boast in — I speak like a

fool — I will also boast about. 22. Are they Hebrews? So am I. Are they Israelites? So am I. Are they the seed of Abraham? So am I.

For the rest of the chapter, Paul begins to "boast" like never before. However, unlike his enemies, Paul boasts in the Lord. The super apostles appealed to their Jewish heritage for ministerial credibility. Paul unfolds his Hebrew certificate as well. One would have difficulty finding another person more Jewish than Paul. He received personal mentorship from the Hebrew sage Gamaliel (Acts 22:3) and most likely served on the Sanhedrin at one point.

23. Are they servants of Christ? — I speak like a fool — I excel over them in that; I have worked harder, been imprisoned more often, had my back opened more severely, and faced death time and again.

After cementing his lineage, Paul catalogues his sufferings endured for Christ. Aspiring, young preachers sometimes view ministry as a context for fame, fortune, and ease. Yet from the day of his conversion, the Lord proclaimed "Paul must suffer great things for my name's sake" (Acts 9:16). By very definition, ministry (διακονία/diakonia) means, not the accumulation of accolades and adoring fans, but "service" to others. The service of ministry moves far past the minister's comfort zone, calendar, or starry-eyed aspirations. Jesus left the comfort and praise of heaven; "the Son of Man came not to be served but to serve others and to give his life as the necessary payment for the release of many" (Mark 10:45). This involved becoming obedient, not merely to the point of discomfort, but to a nearly unimaginably difficult death (Phil. 2:8).

Satan has convinced many to see the sacrificial life as one of dreadful drudgery. The one bearing the very name "Truth" states otherwise by saying, "Whoever finds their life will lose it, and whoever loses their life for my sake will find it" (Matt. 10:39 NIV). Only through death to self does one discover life wrapped in their true, God-ordained identity. The one modeling a perfect example of sacrifice received, after His death, an equal degree of exaltation (Phil. 2:9). Paul's life of surrender afforded him open hands for grasping the greatness of God's blessings.

Paul's listing of hardships does not paint the picture of a sick, broke, depressed person. Rather than beating him down, these immense troubles caused Paul to more fully appreciate his "more than conqueror" state of being. The development of perseverance brought Paul into treasure rooms most never walk into. It also brought forth in him an iron chin immune to the devil's most powerful knockout blows. Attacks that would floor most only caused Paul to shrug, look Satan in the eyes, and ask, "Is that your best shot?"

Through it all, Paul understands the vital role perseverance plays in both character development and reward procurement. Thus, he confidently tells the church that "our light and momentary troubles are achieving for us an eternal glory that far outweighs them all" (2 Cor. 4:17 NIV). Regarding overall service in the face of difficulty, he claims to have περισσοτέρως (perissoteros), or "totally outdone," his accusers.

Next, Paul lists more specific troubles wherein he has far surpassed his opponents. He has been locked in prison far more frequently. With a nearly complete absence of light, ventilation, and adequate food, Roman φυλακή (phulake), "jail," conditions proved remarkably harsher than present-day American prisons. While incarcerated, Paul refused to play the role of victim. Instead, he called himself "a prisoner of Jesus Christ" (Eph. 3:1, 4:1; 2 Tim. 1:18; Philem. 1:1, 9). With this unstoppable attitude, wherever Paul found himself locked up, the Spirit broke out in miraculous manifestations.

In addition to the authorities locking him up, they also opened him up with "stripes" on his back, a term from the Greek πληγή (plege), meaning "a severe blow." A phonetic pronunciation of πληγή reveals the English word "plague," another of the term's meanings. Plaguing a person with such blows could be a fate worse than death.

The Roman government meted out this torturous tactic in an effort to extract information from tight lipped suspects. Two well-trained soldiers took turns raining down horrific fury from a leather lash. This whip, called a *flagrum*, proved exceptionally sadistic. It had a main stem with up to nine leather braches. Attached at the end of each branch were lead balls from which projected either nails, fragments of animal bones, or shards of glass. After removing the victim's shirt, vengeance began tearing into the recipients back, buttocks, and occasionally upper legs.[2] The flagrum rendered one's back nearly unrecognizable while undergoing whipping. The savage removal of skin and muscle tissue caused the ripped flesh to quiver noticeably. All of this left the victim with a lifelong roadmap of scars. Even the hardened psyches of battle-hardened Roman soldiers occasionally bristled at enacting this form of punishment.

24. Five separate times I received forty lashes from the Jews, minus one.

Amazingly, Paul endured this, not once, but multiple times. Scars upon scars revealed layers of love for the Lamb of God. If this were not enough, Paul ends verse 23 with the assertion that, for him, the possibility of death remains a ubiquitous reality. Paul received floggings from "the Jews" five separate times. Out of compassion for the offender, the law of Moses set the maximum number of stripes at forty (Deut. 25:33). Due to their relevance, two Jewish customs deserve discussion here. First, as guardrail preventing one from going over the maximum of forty stripes, leaders set in place the number thirty-nine. Also, a custom demanded for a pre examination regarding the physical fitness of the one slated for flogging. Those deemed ill or weak would receive a lesser amount proportionate to their ability to withstand the blows. The fact that Paul regularly received the maximum amount undercuts the foolish myth that Paul walked around weak and sickly.

25. Three times I was beaten with rods, once I was stoned, I was shipwrecked three times, I spent a night and a day in the open ocean.

While scourging took place in both Roman and Jewish circles, the "beating with rods" remained solely within Roman governmental boundaries. High-ranking bodyguards called *lictors* watched over powerful magistrates. These lictors carried with them bundles of birch rods tied with leather straps called *fasces*.[3] Fasces signified the unified power of Roman government in general and the local power of the magistrate in particular. A fasces also contained an axe bound with the rods. This spoke of the magistrate's authority to carry out, if necessary, capital punishment via beheading. Occasionally, in a show of governmental strength, magistrates would order lictors to enact punishment by beating an offender with the rods comprising the fasces.

Rome never enacted this form of discipline on noncitizens. It served as a kind of gracious, albeit severe warning for a citizen to shape up and get with the program. Magistrates, via lictors, could beat citizens with rods on the spot without a trial.

Causing civil unrest would certainly result in one receiving this punishment. While in Philippi, Paul and Silas unintentionally enacted a stir both politically and economically. The deliverance of a female psychic caused the profit margin of her owners to plummet. They responded by violently taking Paul and Silas before the local magistrate. True to form, "the magistrates ordered them stripped and beaten with wooden rods" (Acts 16:22).

In addition to enduring severe beatings, a confederation of Paul's enemies stoned him to death in Lystra (Acts 14:19). Later in chapter 12, Paul explains that this conglomeration of opponents made up his "thorn in the flesh."

Paul experienced the perils of shipwreck three times and spent at least twenty-four hours in the sea. The word βυθῷ (buthos), meaning "deep water," places him adrift for an extended period of time in the open ocean. Paul covers a large spectrum of locations (rivers, cities, desolate places, and the sea) and people groups (Jew and Gentiles) where danger assailed him with great force.

26. I have been subjected to constant travels. [While traveling] I have been in danger from rivers, in danger from bandits, in danger from the Jews, in danger from the Gentiles, in danger while in the city, in danger while in the wilderness, and in danger while at sea. I have also been in danger from

false brothers [those claiming to follow Christ though they do not].

One of the toughest kind of attacks came from ψευδαδέλφοις (pseudadelphos), or "false brothers." This word displays the same prefix as the Greek word for "false apostles," ψευδαπόστολοι (pseudapostolos). Like their public ministry counterparts, these false believers actively veil selfish intentions in costumes made from the fabric of false spirituality.

Their true colors come out when one of two things happen: correction or times requiring hard work without recognition. If someone corrects a false brother, the smoke and mirrors quickly disappear and their insecurities takes center stage. Likewise, if a task requires consistent effort with no public recognition, their resolve rapidly wilts away. Jesus explained that hypocrites (costume wearers) do things "to be seen by others" (Matt. 6:5). If people praise them, false brothers will run to the task. If not, like blisters on a hand, they show up after the work is done.

27. I have worked tirelessly. [In the process,] I have often endured sleepless nights, gone without food, fasted frequently, and experienced extreme cold due to not having proper clothing

During certain legs of his missionary travels, Paul went without sleep, food, water, and decent shelter. However, during these times he gained a new depth on knowing God's provision. During sleepless nights, he walked hand in hand with the one who never slumbers. While thirsty, he drank deeply from the water of life. While hungry, he ate the bread of heaven. While without shelter, he abode in the shadow of the Almighty. The one telling believers, "My God will supply all your needs in proportion to his abundant supply in glory by means of Christ Jesus" speaks from experience at the deepest level.

28. In addition to all of those things, I have the daily task of overseeing all the churches [I planted].

In addition to the pressures from enemies of the cross, Paul had planted in his soul a real concern for all the churches he planted. Whenever a church member experienced pain, Paul felt that pain. If someone walked away from the things of God, it angered him. On the other hand, when someone experienced victory, Paul shared directly in their joys. This is in contrast to a two-faced leader who latches onto those soaring and either avoids or runs from those sinking in pain.

29. Who is weak and I don't together with them feel weak? Who is led into sin and I don't burn with anger?

However, Paul sees love as a two-sided coin that rejoices with those who rejoice, but also weeps with those who weep (Rom. 12:15). Indeed, regarding the church, "If one part suffers, all the parts suffer with it, and if one part is honored, all the parts are glad" (1 Cor. 12:26 NLT).

30. If I am pressured to boast, I will boast about my weaknesses. 31. The God and father of the Lord Jesus, the one praised forever, knows that I am not lying.

In preparation for the content of chapter 12, Paul again talks about boasting about his "infirmities." As detailed earlier, to translate ἀσθενείας (astheneo) as "infirmities" in 2 Corinthians runs contrary to the entire flow of the letter. Furthermore, the word often means "without strength" or "unimpressive." Here, he says, "If I have to brag, I will highlight my limitations outside the Lord." Paul knows that in himself, without Jesus, he has nothing to boast of. However, when Paul considers the great things God has done through someone so "unimpressive," he stands in amazement.

The Lord takes delight in ordering things in such a manner. He deliberately "chose things the world considers foolish in order to shame those who think they are wise. And he chose things that are powerless to shame those who are powerful" (1 Cor. 1:27 NLT).[4]

32. In Damascus, the governor under King Aretas had the entire city surrounded to capture me. 33. However, I was put

in a basket and let down from a window in the city wall, slipping through his grasp.

Curiously, Paul ends this section by retelling an event, also seen in Acts 9:22–25, from the infancy stage of his ministry. Perhaps he includes this testimony to showcase God's protection from the beginning of his Christian life until the present.

12:1–21 The Power of Weakness

12:1–6

1. Boasting like this doesn't really give me an advantage. Nevertheless, I continue on by talking about visions and revelations from the Lord.

Paul shifts his focus from trials to supernatural "visions and revelations." The word translated "visions" comes from the Greek term ὀπτασία (*optasia*) meaning "something seen as a result of another showing themselves." When a believer experiences a vision, this means the Lord sought to supernaturally reveal a portion of Himself. Furthermore, unlike pagan visons often fixating on the experience itself, God desires to impart a ἀποκαλύψεις (*apokalupsis*), the "uncovering of something veiled" or "showing forth of a truth previously unknown." The title for the book of Revelation comes from this word. Ironically, a book whose very title speaks of uncovering remains shrouded in mystery for many believers.

2. In Christ, fourteen years ago, I was grabbed hold of and taken all the way to the third heaven. Whether I was in my body or out of my body, I'm not certain — God knows. 3. Indeed, only God knows whether I was in or out of the body.

Paul explains that he was "grabbed hold of and taken all the way to the third heaven." The atmosphere above earth comprises the first heaven and stellar space the second. Beyond space and time lies the third heaven. The genitive preposition ἕως (*heos*) conveys the meaning "as far as" or "all the way until" the third heaven.

Just as stellar space remains veiled by the earth's atmosphere, another kind of veil shrouds the third heaven from plain sight. At times, the gift of "discerning of spirits" affords its recipient a look behind the veil. The operation of this gift in Paul, during this particular instance, proved so overwhelming that he grew unaware of his physical body.

The Lord either physically transported him to heaven or his spirit went while his body remained on earth.

4. I was caught, grabbed hold of, and taken up to Paradise and heard words so astonishing they cannot find matching expression in human words, things a man is not permitted to speak.

Once in the third heaven, Paul "hears" things. The word translated "hear" comes from the Greek term ἀκούω (akouo) meaning "hear," "comprehend," and "obey." The force of ἀκούω often wanes a bit when coming over into the more generic English "hear." Paul listens, processes, and gives his heart over to what he has heard.

Nevertheless, for two reasons, he cannot share what he has heard. First, the Lord did not grant him permission to share the particular revelation. Those always itching to share their latest divine revelation display either an innocent lack of maturity or a propensity toward nongenuine visions. Wisdom instructs those receiving visions to exercise care regarding the delivery of that revelation. Oftentimes, the Lord will have a person hold on to a revelation for a later date, sometimes several years later. The Spirit will also lead a person to exercise care regarding who should hear their revelation. Even the best visions shared either too soon or with the wrong crowd can have adverse effects. For an example, just ask Joseph.

Of course, sometimes, God will commission a person for immediate and large scale vision proclamation. When the Lord does so, to hold back amounts to stark disobedience. After walking such a path, the prophet Jeremiah said, "[God's Word is] like a fire in my bones! I am worn out trying to hold it in! (Jer. 20:9 NLT). Paul explains that even if he had permission, he lacks the vocabulary to express the vision's content. This is quite an admission from one of the most well-educated men of his day.

5. That experience merits boasting. However, merely about myself I will not boast, except about my weaknesses. 6. Even if I do choose to boast, I would not be speaking as a fool, for

I would be speaking the truth [speaking about things that actually happened to me]. But I hold back so that no one might perceive me as greater than what my life and message reveal.

Paul notes that the experience would certainly merit a great deal of boasting. Furthermore, he has had many other supernatural revelations. However, in order to not draw attention to himself, he will not speak more about them. While visions played an integral part in Paul's life, his ministry stood on the foundation of the written Word and serving others in selfless love. Ministries built solely on new revelations always require one more to maintain forward momentum.

12:7–10

7. I have received such amazing revelations from God. Therefore, in order that I might not be highly exalted, I was given a thorn in the flesh, a messenger of Satan. [He was sent] so that he might treat me roughly, in order that I might not be highly exalted.

Whenever God uses a person in spectacular ways, the step from "Look at the great things God did through me" to "Look at the great me" proves deceptively short. By placing ὑπεραίρομαι (huperairomai), meaning "to highly exalt oneself," in the subjunctive mood, Paul shows that a move into arrogance remains a matter of choice rather than inevitability, thus the translation, "lest I should be exalted." This word describes the ultimate example of pride witnessed in the maniacal Antichrist who "exalts himself above all that is called God or that is worshiped, so that he sits as God in the temple of God, showing himself that he is God" (2 Thess. 2:4 NKJ).

In order to save Paul from delusions of grandeur, a reality check mechanism sits firmly in place. He calls this instrument a "thorn in the flesh." The word translated as "thorn" comes from the Greek term σκόλοψ (skolops). In Classical Greek, this word meant "something pointed." By New Testament times, it had evolved to signify "something causing a severe annoyance." Of course, due to both their pointiness and annoying characteristics, Greeks also assigned the word to both "thorns" and "splinters." The English colloquial expression "like a rock stuck in my shoe" conveys a similar force.

Strangely, some view the thorn sent to Paul as physical illness. Yet none of the entire context of 2 Corinthians, the immediate context of chapter 12, or the meaning of σκόλοψ speak to anything regarding sickness or disease. Paul suffering hardships for Christ in no way includes taking on himself things Jesus has already taken away.

Perhaps the phrase thorn "in the flesh" causes some to see this splinter as physical illness. Such a view results from misappropriating an artificial narrowness to the word σάρξ (sarx), translated as "flesh." Many claim σάρξ categorically means "selfish sinful nature." Without question, Paul often uses the term in that manner. However, in other places in Scripture, writers use σάρξ when speaking of the physical body. Words take on meaning in context. For example, the English word "pot" displays a fluidity in various contexts. The statement, "The word 'pot' means a container for planting flowers" is an accurate assessment. However, the assertion, "the word pot always means a container for planting flowers" proves false. "Pot" can also mean "a vessel for cooking."

The same linguistic principle applies to σάρξ. If σάρξ always means "selfish nature" the New Testament contains a real theological conundrum. When describing the very incarnation of the Son of God, John states, "The eternal Word became flesh (σάρξ)." Knowing that σάρξ can mean either "selfish nature" or "the physical body," one must examine context to discern its meaning in a particular passage. Paul weaves the theme of laying down selfishness in favor of sacrificial service throughout 2 Corinthians. In the immediate context of chapter 12, he has spoken strongly about not "elevating himself." Right after this statement, he mentions the "splinter" stuck in his ego. Whenever the temptation for self-exaltation presents itself, this splinter keeps him from boasting in himself. Furthermore, the sentence's grammatical construction overwhelmingly supports this conclusion. The phrase "thorn in the flesh" sits sandwiched between two identical uses of ὑπεραίρωμαι (huperairomai), or "self-exaltation." The thorn came in the form of a "messenger of Satan intent on making life tough for me."

The term often translated "buffet" comes from the Greek word κολαφίζω (kolaphizo), meaning "to hit" or "treat roughly." Gospel writers used this word to describe the beating Jesus took prior to His scourging and crucifixion (Matt. 26:67, Mark 14:65). Peter encourages believers to endure by saying, "What credit is it if, when you are beaten (κολαφίζω) for your faults, you take it patiently? But when you do good and suffer, if you take it patiently, this is commendable before God" (1 Pet. 2:20 NKJ). Paul regularly endured severe beatings by a confederation of Jews obsessed with persecuting him. As discussed above, they stoned him to death in Lystra (Acts 14:19). No matter where Paul went, this splinter of persecution followed.

8. Concerning this matter, I had serious discussions with the Lord three separate times, asking Him [each time] to take it away from me [get it out of my life].

On three separate occasions, he asked the Lord to take divine tweezers to the problem.

9. But he said to me, "My grace is more than enough for you. My power works best during times of weakness [when you have no natural solution]." That's why I will boast even more about my weaknesses, so that [at that moment] the power of Christ can work through me [show forth an even fuller expression].

The same answer came back each time: "My grace is more than enough!" God said to Paul, "You will be fine, for my power reaches a fuller potential in those depending on me." The power that created and upholds the universe finds a fuller expression when opposition arises. Commercial airliners have much more power available than a typical takeoff requires. When a plane carries a heavier load than normal, the pilot pushes on the throttle and releases additional power. The same principle applies to the power of God. In times of heavy difficulty, the release of power increases accordingly. In fact, the greater the difficulty, the more explosive the power. Jesus reminded Paul, "In the course of you advancing my kingdom, no manner of opposition will ever overpower my power within you!"

Therefore, Paul says, "I take great joy in boasting about my weaknesses. For this means I will see a greater release of God's power." Darkness provides an opportunity for light, blindness for sight, abandonment for security, and opposition for victory.

The believer need not have the answers in the natural. One can stand before a crowd of thousands with only five loaves of bread and two fish and call them to dinner. Times of natural inadequacy plus faith equals the release of miracle working power.

10. Therefore, I get excited in weaknesses, in insults, outward pressures, persecutions, and difficulties while serving Christ. For when I am weak, then I am powerful [made strong with power to do the impossible].

Paul sums up the matter with the confession, "At the very point when my own ability is weakest, I am exponentially stronger in God." It bears noting that this law does not work for those intent only on living for self. Paul does not say, "In the course of trying to get God to do things my way, I am strong." Instead, he shouts, "I take pleasure in my weaknesses and in the insults, hardships, persecutions, and troubles that I suffer for Christ" (2 Cor. 12:10 NLT).

12:11–21

11. You have forced my hand to become foolish by boasting like this. You should have been commending me; for I am in no way inferior to these "super apostles," even though I am a nobody.

Paul reiterates how he would have preferred to not hold forth his credentials. The Corinthians had, by giving an ear to the "super apostles," forced his hand.

12. I consistently performed the signs of an apostle in your presence: signs, wonders, and miracles.

They should have realized that his walking in signs and wonders coupled with his character spoke volumes. The σημεῖα (semeion), or "signs," of an apostle signifies the proof of one being sent. Anyone can claim apostleship on a website, business card, or banner. However, people cannot send themselves. By very definition, a sent one must be sent by another.

In the New Testament, an ἀπόστολος (apostolos) means "one sent with authority to accomplish the will of a superior." The commission of apostleship, while recognized by others, comes directly from the head of the church. True apostles have a dramatic encounter with Jesus whereupon they receive their commission.

The proof of apostleship Paul speaks of here comes in two forms: the power to plant new churches and the ability to work signs, wonders, and miracles. Any minister not possessing these credentials does not bear the scriptural stamp of an authentic apostle. Those sent forth by their own greed to reap money from already established churches do not fit the bill. Ministers seeking to prop up deep insecurities by cloaking themselves with titles do not pass the test. In addition to receiving a commission; planting churches; and working signs, wonders, and miracles; true apostles project, above all else, the character trait displayed by the apostle of our faith: love. A commission can be embellished. Satan can enable one to perform "lying signs and wonders" (2 Thess. 2:9). A gifted communicator can gather a group of people and call that gathering a church. However, one can never fake sacrificial love.

13. In what way are you inferior to any of the other churches, except that I was never a [financial] burden to you? Forgive me for doing you this injustice!

Paul exhibited further evidence of his love by not burdening the church with offerings. He sarcastically asks them, "Forgive me for offending you in this."

14. Now I am coming to you for a third time, and I will not be a burden to you. I do not seek after your material possessions, I want you. For sure, children don't save up for their parents, but the parents do so for their children. 15. I will most gladly spend all I have, including my very life, for you. [I do this] even if the more I love you, the less you love me. 16. Even though that's the case, I did not burden you. But some think I was clever and deceitfully trapped you. 17. Did I exploit you by means of those I sent to you? 18. I urged Titus [to go] and sent another brother along with him. Did Titus exploit you? Didn't we walk step-by-step together in the same spirit? 19. Again, do you think that we are defending ourselves to you? We tell you in Christ before God; we do everything, dear friends, in order to build you up.

While his opponents see the Corinthians as an income stream, Paul seeks to give rather than take. Even in the natural, "children don't provide for their parents. Rather, parents provide for their children" (2 Cor. 12:14 NLT).

Paul, Titus, and others Paul sent to Corinth all conducted themselves with the utmost integrity. They may not have the flash, outward magnetism, and clever sounding teachings of the "super apostles." However, they have proven their love. Oftentimes, people gravitating toward "the new teaching" view themselves as zealous. Casting aside those with proven ministries in favor of those representing the latest Christian trends reveals, not godly zeal, but adolescent immaturity. Teenagers often view the loving gestures of caring parents as manipulative, outdated, and unnecessary restrictions. "What do mom and dad know, they are so old and uncool." With the response of a loving spiritual father, Paul says, "We tell you this as Christ's servants, and with God as our witness. Everything we do, dear friends, is to strengthen you" (2 Cor. 12:19 NLT).

20. For I am afraid that when I come, I won't find you living like I desire, and you will not like how I respond. Perhaps there will be strife, jealousy, outbursts of anger, selfish ambition, slander, gossip, overinflated egos, and out of control behavior.

Paul has a great concern that the Corinthians may have regressed into fleshly living. He never stands under a delusion that his preaching alone will always result in obedience. Wisdom accounts for the power of free will to toss away progress in the pursuit of self-centeredness. Paul's then presents a list of possible traps. The first four words used also occur in the string of "works of the flesh" featured in Galatians 5:20.

While several of these behaviors look very similar to one another, they possess distinctness. He first speaks of ἔρις (eris) meaning "discordant viewpoints leading to arguments." Next, Paul speaks of ζῆλος (zelos) signifying "zealously clinging to a divisive opinion or a group holding to a divisive opinion." He then, moves to the oft used word θυμοίt (humos), connoting "anger" or "rage." What follows on the heels of rage is "electioneering for a selfish cause" (ἐριθείαι/eritheiai). Angry, divisive people campaign for others to join in their cause.

When recruiting followers, such people use two kinds of evil speaking. Paul calls the first one "slander" (καταλαλιαί/katalalia) and the other "gossip" (ψιθυρισμοί/psithurismos). The former centers around completely false accusations of gross character flaws, and the latter regards pointing out minor yet true imperfections. Assailants intend for both arrows to kill their target: one quickly and the other slowly. Slander says, "The pastor is having an affair" when he most certainly is not. Gossip highlights a real situation and then magnifies it far past reality. For example, "I saw the pastor's wife get angry with her kids" — a true incident — therefore, "she is a hateful person who needs to be corrected by her husband." Those hurling the stones of slander and gossip view themselves, not simply as "right," but far more correct than others. They campaign to gather other "spiritual" people around the cause. When they look in the mirror, they see a spiritual giant rather than an insecure, hurting person. Paul captures this truth in the word φυσιώσεις (phusiosis) meaning "arrogant or puffed up."

All of these ingredients taken together form ἀκαταστασίαι (akatastasia), or "chaos," within the group. The enemy peddles this scheme to fleshly people in order to upend God's order in families, businesses, governments, and churches.

James ties several of these same words together and, like Paul, concludes that they result in ἀκαταστασίαι. In so doing, James exposes one's heart as the cause of this dysfunction. Under inspiration of the Spirit, James writes, "If you embrace jealousy [zealously hold to a divisive position] (ζῆλον) and selfish agendas [campaign for a selfish cause] (ἐριθείαν) in your heart, you are lying to yourself and covering up the truth. This 'wisdom'[you think you are right] is not coming from above, but is earthly, physical, and demonic. For wherever there is jealously [zealously holding to a divisive position] (ζῆλον) and selfish agendas [campaign for a selfish cause] (ἐριθείαν), there is also surely disorder (ἀκαταστασίαι) and every evil deed. (James 3:14–16).

21. I am concerned that when I come back, God will humble me in your presence, and I will be grieved concerning many who have sinned before and have still not repented of their uncleanness, sexual sin, and shameless lusts in which they regularly engaged in.

In the chapter's final verse, Paul shows a stark concern for their lifestyles. At first glance, this admonition seems out of place. However, Paul knows that those embracing strange teachers most often already hold tightly to aberrant behavior. False teaching resonates with false living. His concluding remarks serve as a hinge upon which the door opens into the book's final chapter.

13:1-14 Final Thoughts

13:1–6

1. This is the third time I am coming to you. [I follow God's Word which says] "Every word should be confirmed by the mouth of two or three witnesses." 2. I have already given you a warning while with you the second time. Now, I am telling you again while not present with you. I write to those who have previously sinned and the others: when I return, I won't spare anyone 3. because you seek proof that Christ is speaking though me. He is not weak in dealing with you, but powerful among you.

Were Paul's words in chapter 13 spoken in many of today's churches, dimple marks would fill the sanctuaries from jaws hitting floors. He speaks with a tone of authority only resident in those caring nothing for the praises of men. Paul does, however, care deeply for the Corinthian believers. He begins by laying out his care in following scriptural steps when dealing with recalcitrant offenders. He alludes to the old covenant practice of involving two or three witnesses (Deut. 17:6). Jesus established this principle for new covenant church discipline by laying out the following instructions: "If your brother sins against you, go and tell him his fault between you and him alone. If he hears you, you have gained your brother. But if he will not hear, take with you one or two more, that by the mouth of two or three witnesses every word may be established. And if he refuses to hear them, tell it to the church. But if he refuses even to hear the church, let him be to you like a heathen and a tax collector" (Matt. 18:15–17 NKJ).

In this first verse he quotes Deuteronomy, wherein the Lord establishes a threefold layer of accountability from individual to an entire church. Paul has gone above and beyond regarding these instructions. Although not the pastor in Corinth, Paul had true apostolic authority. This came from both his apostolic ministry gift in general and, more germane to this letter, his founding of the church in Corinth. As the church's leader, people had, after taking the other steps detailed in Matthew 18, come to him many times regarding conflicts in Corinth. In response, he has already both traveled to and written Corinth several times.

In today's church culture, the concept of "disfellowshipping" someone seems exceptionally odd at best and unthinkably harsh at worst. However, this practice remained a regular part of Israelite, Greco-Roman, and early church cultures. Banishment from the camp of Israel stood as a punishment worse than physical death. Secular Greek culture embraced the practice of sending away those refusing to let go of destructive behavior. Greeks and Romans found a great deal of their purpose manifested within their community. The famous Greek poet Alcaeus encapsulated this foundational value of society when writing: "Not houses finely roofed or the stones of walls well builded, nay nor canals and dockyards make the city, but men able to use their opportunity." Greeks viewed those sent away from the community as less than human.

Of course, the essential nature of community finds unforgettable expression in the New Testament in the body of Christ with its many members. Today's church dare not consign the truth of church discipline to a place locked up in the first century. Those rightfully contending that the ministry gifts revealed in Ephesians and gifts of the Spirit detailed in 1 Corinthians 12 and 14 have not "passed away" must also have the courage to see the church discipline of 1 and 2 Corinthians as viable for today. This discipline is not simply a cloudy practice of the early church to be studied, but a clear responsibility for every church to embody.

When addressing sinful behavior, Paul uses the phrase, "I have already told you once, now I am telling you again." This translation stems from two different forms of the Greek word προλέγω (prolegeo). This term consists of the word λέγω (lego) meaning "to speak" and the prefix πρό (pro) meaning "beforehand." Interestingly, when rebuking the Galatians for the "works of the flesh," Paul employs two forms of προλέγω as well. He writes, "Let me tell you again, as I have before, that anyone living that sort of life will not inherit the kingdom of God" (Gal. 5:21 NLT). In both cases, Paul speaks of carrying out proper protocol for church discipline. Some view an adherence to order as inherently contrary to being led by the Spirit. While true for frivolous, man-made tradition, the rule does not apply to instructions laid out in God's Word. For Paul, any order mapped out by Scripture creates a context for a greater moving of the Spirit. Having covered the bases, he speaks clearly about his intentions to clean house upon arrival.

Throughout his letters, Paul has used the word ἀσθενέω (astheneo), meaning "unimpressive," to describe himself. Now, in the context of church discipline, he says that Christ is not ἀσθενέω, but powerful in his dealings with them. The desire for a "powerful move of God" remains a noble one. However, power-filled moves of God flow to every aspect of church life, including discipline. Just ask Ananias and Sapphira.

4. Although he was crucified in weakness, he now lives by the power of God. In the same way, we are also weak in Him, but we will live with Him by the power of God concerning you. 5. Examine yourselves to discern if you are abiding in the faith. Put yourselves through the test. Don't you realize that Jesus Christ is in you — unless you, in some way, do not pass the test. 6. But I trust that you know from experience that we have not failed the test.

Although Christ was crucified in weakness, He now lives in power. Likewise, while they have seen Paul's meekness, they are about to see his severity. Few believers today have any comprehension of the severity of God. To many, God consistently displays a chipper attitude no matter what occurs. Any talk of wrath garners the charge of "legalists" and one who "just doesn't understand mercy." However, without wrath, mercy loses its meaning altogether. Scripture exhorts believers to "Notice how God is both kind and severe" (Rom. 11:22 NLT).

13:7–10

7. Now we pray to God that you won't do the wrong thing [be rebelling against our authority]; not so that we might appear

genuine, but that you should do what is honorable even if it makes it look like we have failed the test. 8. For we can do nothing contrary to the truth, but only for the truth.

Paul prays for the Corinthians to get their house in order before he arrives. Like a master chess player, Paul accurately anticipates the moves of his opponents. If he threatens discipline, and the Corinthians repent before his arrival, he cannot justly exercise corrective measures. His enemies will perceive this as floundering. They will then seek to confirm to the church their former charges about Paul being wishy-washy in decision making. Nevertheless, his love for the Corinthians shines through in the matter.

9. Indeed, we rejoice when we are weak and you [as a result] are strong. We pray for you to mature. 10. For this reason, I am writing these things while absent in order that when I come I won't have to exercise severity while using the authority the Lord gave me for building up and not tearing down.

He easily agrees to pay the price of playing the fool in the eyes of his accusers if it means the church will repent. His concern lies not with propping up his leadership approval rating with the masses, but the spiritual growth of the church. Like a true spiritual father, he tells them, "We are fine appearing weak if that helps you to truly be strong; we also pray for your spiritual maturity." Like any good parent, he has no hesitation using his authority to correct. However, he would much rather use it to build them up instead of to tear down edifices built by the enemy.

13:11–14

11. Finally brothers and sisters, farewell. Rejoice! Be maturing. Be comforted. Be likeminded. Be at peace. Then the God of peace will be with you.

Paul ends this labor of love with a profoundly simple, yet simply profound confession of unifying peace upon the church.

12. Greet each other with a holy kiss. 13. All the saints here send their greetings.

He then urges them to "greet one another with a 'holy kiss ($\varphi i\lambda\eta\mu\alpha$/ *philema*).'" In addition to here, Paul encourages this form of greeting three other times in his letters and Peter does so once (Rom. 16:16, 1 Cor. 16:20, 1 Thess. 5:26, 1 Peter 5:14). In the New Testament world, this very common gesture had no sexual connotation whatsoever. The "holy kiss" consisted of a quick kiss on the side of the face.

Today, in many parts of the world, this form of greeting still occurs as a gesture of friendship. In the American church, the practice remains taboo. When one considers the Puritan heritage of the United States, this comes as no surprise. In his commentary on this verse, well known eighteenth century Puritan writer Matthew Henry notes that, "the sacred rite of a kiss of charity, which was then used, but has long been disused, to prevent all occasions of wantonness and impurity, in the more declining and degenerate state of the church."[1]

14. May the grace of the Lord Jesus Christ, and the love of God, and the communion of the Holy Spirit be with you all.

In his final sentence, Paul's includes a laconic, power-packed statement concerning the Trinity by saying, "May the grace of the Lord Jesus Christ, and the love of God, and the communion of the Holy Spirit be with you all."

Notes

Authorship

1. Frederick W. Danker, *II Corinthians* (Minneapolis: Augsburg, 1989), 13.

2. James D. Hernando, "2 Corinthians," *Full Life Bible Commentary to the New Testament*, ed. F.L. Arrington and Roger Stronstad (Grand Rapids: Zondervan, 1999), 915–62. It is also noteworthy that neither the *New International Commentary on the New Testament* nor the *World Biblical Commentary* volumes on 2 Corinthians deal with authorship theories.

3. Hernando, "2 Corinthians," 915.

4. Ibid.

5. A.T. Robertson, *A Grammar of the Greek New Testament in Light of Historical Research* (Nashville: Broadman Press, 1934), 128.

6. For an excellent argument that Paul changes his style to fit the occasion, see A.B. Spencer's *Paul's Literary Style: A Stylistic and Historical Comparison of II Corinthians 11: 16–12: 13, Romans 8:9–39, and Philippians 3:2–4:13* (Jackson, MS: Evangelical Theology Society, 1984).

7. Hernando, "2 Corinthians," 915.

8. Ibid; In 2 Cor., this pastoral concern is also seen in 1:3–11; 2: 1–4,5–11, 14; 6: 11–13; 7:2–4; 8:16; 11:1–4; 12:14–21

9. Ibid.

10. Danker, *II Corinthians*, 13.

11. Hernando, "2 Corinthians," 915.

12. Paul Barnett, The Epistle to the Corinthians, *New International Commentary on the New Testament* (Grand Rapids: Eerdmans, 1997), 9; Danker, *II Corinthians*, 14.

13. Barnett, *Epistle to the Corinthians*, 9.

14. Ibid, 10.

15. Hernando, "2 Corinthians," 916.

16. Ralph P. Martin, *2 Corinthians*, World Biblical Commentary (Waco: Word, 1986), xxxiii.

17. Danker, *II Corinthians*, 13; For a laconic outline of these events see: Hernando, "2 Corinthians," 915–17.

18. See 1 Cor. 16:10; Acts 19:22.

19. Hernando, "2 Corinthians," 916.

20. Ibid; Barnett, *Epistle to the Corinthians*, 13.

21. This designation may refer to either 1) the Jerusalem apostles so esteemed by Paul's opponents or 2) the opponents themselves. Paul's opponents were certainly self-inflated to the point of bursting.

22. Barnett, *Epistle to the Corinthians*, 13.

23. Hernando, "2 Corinthians," 920.

24. Ibid.

25. For a thorough treatment in favor of the opponents being Judaizers, see R.P. Martin, "The Opponents of Paul in 2 Corinthians: An Old Issue Revisited," in *Tradition and Interpretation in the New Testament*, ed. E.E. Ellis (Grand Rapids: Baker, 1987).

26. Ben Witherington III, *Conflict and Community in Corinth: A Social-Rhetorical Commentary on 1 and 2 Corinthians* (Grand Rapids: Eerdmans, 1995), 346.

27. Danker, *II Corinthians*, 25.

28. Hernando, "2 Corinthians," 921.

29. Barnett, *Epistle to the Corinthians*, 34 n. 139.

30. Stephen Smalley, *1, 2, 3 John*, World Biblical Commentary (Waco: Word, 1984), xxv.

31. Ibid.

32. Witherington, *Conflict*, 20.

33. Witherington notes that the Corinthians "appear to have been better off than the members of some of Paul's other congregations." *Conflict*, 22–3.

34. David A. DeSilva, *The Credentials of an Apostle: Paul's Gospel in 2 Corinthians 1–7* (North Richland Hills, TX: Bibal Press, 1998), 49.

35. Barnett, *Epistle to the Corinthians*, 38.

3:1–18 The Weighty Glory of the New Covenant

1. For classic arguments for and against the discontinuity of the testaments, see Claus Westermann, ed., *Essays on Old Testament Hermeneutics* (Richmond, VA: 1963). Also, For a somewhat dated but well-written treatment on this subject, see David L. Baker, *Two Testaments: One Bible* (Downers Grove, Ill: IVP, 1976).

2. The author of this commentary comes from a Jewish family and loves his Hebraic heritage. However, in no way does he view himself more enlightened because of it.

3. Witherington, *Conflict*, 378–9.

4. James Denney, *The Second Epistle to the Corinthians* (London: Hodder and Stroughton, 1894), 120.

5. Colin G. Kruse, *Paul's Second Epistle to the Corinthians* (Grand Rapids: Eerdmans, 1987), 92.

6. F.F. Bruce mentions the following quotation from Exodus Rabba xli' (comment Ex. 31:18): "While Israel stood below engraving idols to provoke their Creator to anger. . . , God sat high engraving tablets which would give them life." See F.F. Bruce, *1 and 2 Corinthians*, The New Century Bible Commentary Series (London: Marshall, Morgan, and Scott, 1971), 190.

7. Gordon D. Fee, *God's Empowering Presence: The Holy Spirit in the Letters of Paul* (Peabody, MA: Hendrickson Publishers, 1994) 306.

8. Daniel Wallace, *Greek Grammar Beyond the Basics* (Grand Rapids: Zondervan, 1996), 692–94.

9. lbid., 380.

10. Martin, *2 Corinthians*, 61.

11. Nigel Turner, *Christian Words* (Edinburgh: T&T Clark, 1980), X, 185.

12. lbid., 56.

13. See 1:20, 3:8, 9, 10, 11, 18; 4:4, 6, 15, 17; 6:8; 8:19, 23.

14. Wallace, *Greek Grammar*, 592–94.

15. Hafemann, relying heavily upon TLG (*Thesaurus Linguae Graecae*), makes a strong argument for "abolish." See Scott Hafemann, "The Glory and Veil of Moses in 2 Corinthians 3:7–14: An Example of Paul's Contextual Exegesis of the Old Testament" *Horizons in Biblical Theology 14* (1992), 31–49.

16. See 1 Cor. 1:28, 2:6, 13:8, 10 , 11; Rom. 3:31; Victor P. Furnish, *II Corinthians*, The Anchor Yale Bible Commentaries (New York: Doubleday, 1984), 203; G. Delling, "καταργέω" in *Theological Dictionary of the New Testament*, ed. Gerhard Kittel (Grand Rapids: Eerdmans, 1964), 1:452–4.

17. Barnett, *Epistle to the Corinthians*, 183.

18. J.J. Lias, ed., *The Cambridge University Bible for Schools and Colleges: The Second Epistle to the Corinthians* (London: Cambridge University Press, 1897), 50.

19. Linda Belleville, *Reflections of Glory: Paul's Polemical Use of the Moses-Doxa Tradition in 2 Corinthians 3:1–18* (Sheffield: JSOT Press, 1991), 25.

20. Furnish, *II Corinthians*, 204, 28.

21. See 5:1; 6:7, 14; 9:9, 10; 11:15.

22. Barnett, *Epistle to the Corinthians* ; For examples of covenantal/ forensic uses see: 1 Cor. 1:30, 4:4, 6:11; 2 Cor. 5: 21

23. Martin, *2 Corinthians*, 63 .

24. Fee, *Empowering Presence*, 365.

25. Theodor Brandt, "περισσεύω," in *The New International Dictionary of New Testament Theology*, ed. Colin Brown (Grand Rapids: Zondervan, 1978), 1:728–31.

26. Furnish, *II Corinthians*, 204.

27. Kruse, *The Second Epistle of Paul to the Corinthians* (Grand Rapids: Eerdmans, 1987), 95.

28. Furnish, *II Corinthians*, 205; Alfred Plummer, *A Critical and Exegetical Commentary on the Second Epistle of St. Paul to the Corinthians*, 2nd ed. (Edinburgh: T&T Clark, 1915), 91–2.

29. Furnish, *II Corinthians*, 204.

30. Delling, "ὑπερβάλλω," in *Theological Dictionary of the New Testament*, ed. Gerhard Kittel (Grand Rapids: Eerdmans, 1964), VIII: 520.

31. See 1:8; 3:10, 4:7, 17; 9:14; 12:7.

32. Barnett, *Epistle to the Corinthians*, 187; Plummer, *Critical and Exegetical*, 92.

33. Furnish, *II Corinthians*, 205; Witherington, Conflict, 380.

34. The verb is supplied; being understood from ἐγενήθη.

35. This construction is a dative of measure. Used to show extent of comparison. See Wallace, *Greek Grammar*, 166–7.

36. Denney, *The Second Epistle*, 124; Plummer, *Critical and Exegetical*, 92.

37. In this instance, Carlton Winbery sees little distinction between the two phrases. Carlton Winbery, personal correspondence with author, 13 November 2001.

38. Turner, *Christian Words*, 187.

39. Interestingly, Luke uses the participle form of the same word to describe baby Jesus quietly lying (κείμενον) in a manger (Luke 2:12).

4:1–18 Living Through Dying

1. During the Reformation in Europe, a group arose called the "Anabaptists." This name, thrust upon them by their opponents, resulted from their preaching that only those with a true conversion

experience should enter the waters of baptism. Those baptized as infants had no real ability to comprehend salvation. Therefore, the Anabaptists rebaptized a large number of believing adults.

6:1–18 Genuine Relationship

1. The *pugio's* ability to cause rapid death coupled with its ease of concealment made it the weapon of choice for assassins. Julius Caesar, for example, was killed with several *pugiones*.

2. The Bible contains zero contradictions. A contradiction exemplifies the logical law of noncontradiction. This law states the following: "a" cannot be "a" and "non-a" at the same time and in the same relationship. For example, I cannot be present at a football game and not present at the same time. Even within a game, I cannot be the quarterback and not the quarterback at the same time. Both of these examples exemplify the law of noncontradiction. I can however, be a quarterback and a defensive back on the same team and, if necessary, during the same game while not violating this law.

A paradox is something appearing contradictory. The word comes from the Greek compound word παράδοξο comprised of the verb δοκέω (to seem) and the prefixed preposition παρά (beside). Thus, a παράδοξο is something appearing contradictory when placed alongside a seeming opposite. For example, "you must lose your life to find it." However, upon closer examination, the truth becomes crystal clear. A misunderstanding of this law of logic has caused great confusion regarding the Trinity. In truth, the Trinity is neither a contradiction nor a paradox but a mystery. A mystery concerns something only known in part with much more of it still to learn. In many of his lectures on logic, theologian R.C. Sproul offers a cogent presentation of this subject.

8:1–24 The Grace of Giving

1. The church in Jerusalem had encountered severe persecution bleeding over into their finances. Paul purposes to stem the tide of monetary trouble through receiving an offering from the churches he had already planted.

2. This reveals itself in the mathematical term "isosceles triangle." Such a shape has at least two equal (ἴσος) sides.

9:1–15 Overflowing Abundance

1. The concept of πλεονεξί being comprised of πλέον and ἐξουσία is an idea postulated by me. I have not, to date, heard anyone else offer this idea.

2. The well-known liturgical church term "eulogy" comes from εὐλογία.

11:1–33 Weak Boasting

1. Paul's opponents were not pure Greek sophists. They clearly mixed a Jewish message with sophist methods and success markers.

2. The thought of Jesus shouldering and transporting the massive beam of wood upon his freshly mangled, pulsating back with thighs cut to ribbons seems unfathomable. Yet, out of love for lost humanity, he stepped forward and volunteered for the job.

3. A long history regarding this symbol of power developed among the ancient Etruscans. In modern times, a *fasces* stood as the logo for Mussolini's "fascist" movement in Italy.

4. Origen, a theological giant of the ancient church, championed this line of reasoning. The famous, highly educated, and well-heeled skeptic Celsus sought to characterize Christians as backwoods, uneducated, and generally unimpressive people. He argues that an organization with such nonprominent members has no real legitimacy. In response, Origen surprisingly affirmed the first part of Celsus' charges while turning the latter portion upside down. Origen asserted that many Christians are indeed unimpressive on their own merits. However, the fact that God uses very ordinary people in extraordinary ways ensures that all the glory rises to Him alone.

13:1–14 Final Thoughts

1. Matthew Henry, *Matthew Henry's Commentary on the Whole Bible*, vol. 6, *Acts to Revelation* (McLean, VA: MacDonald Publishing Company, 1985), 646.

Selected Bibliography

Books and Articles

Barrett, C.K. "Opposition in Corinth." *New Testament Studies 17, No. 3* (1971): 233–54.

Barnett, Paul. *The Second Epistle to the Corinthians.* The New International Commentary on the New Testament. Grand Rapids: Eerdmans, 1997.

Beker, J. Christian, *The Triumph of God: The Essence of Paul's Thought.* Translated by Loren T. Stuckenbruck. Minneapolis: Fortress Press, 1990.

Belleville, Linda L. *Reflections of Glory: Paul's Polemical Use of the Moses-Doxa Tradition in 2 Corinthians 3:1–18.* Sheffield: JSOT Press, 1991.

_____. "Tradition or Creation? Paul's Use of the Exodus 34 Tradition 2 Corinthians 3:7–18." *Paul and the Scriptures of Israel.* Edited by Craig. A. Evans and James Sanders, 165–86. Sheffield: JSOT Press, 1993.

Bratcher, Robert G. *A Translators Guide to Paul' s Second Letter to the Corinthians.* New York: United Bible Societies, 1983.

Bruce, F. F. *New Century Bible Commentary: 1 and 2 Corinthians.* The New Century Bible Commentary Series. London: Marshall, Morgan, and Scott, 1971.

Crafton, Jeffrey A. *The Agency of the Apostle: A Dramatic Analysis of Paul's Responses to Conflict in 2 Corinthians*. Sheffield: Sheffield Academic Press, 1991.

Danker, Frederick W. *II Corinthians*. Augsberg Commentary on the New Testament. Minneapolis: Augsburg, 1989.

Denney, James. *The Second Epistle to the Corinthians*. London: Hodder and Stoughton, 1894.

Davies, W.D. *Paul and Rabbinic Judaism: Some Rabbinic Elements in Pauline Theology*. New York: Harper & Row, 1967.

DeSilva, David A. *The Credentials of an Apostle: Paul's Gospel in 2 Corinthians 1–7*. Bibal Monograph Series. North Richland Hills, TX: Bibal Press, 1998.

Dunn, James D.G. *Unity and Diversity in the New Testament: Inquiry into the Character of Earliest Christianity*. 2nd ed. Harrisburg, PA: Trinity Press, 1990.

Fee, Gordon D. *God's Empowering Presence: The Holy Spirit in the Letters of Paul*. Peabody, MA: Hendrickson Publishers, 1994.

Furnish, Victor P. *II Corinthians*. The Anchor Yale Bible Commentaries. New York: Doubleday, 1984.

Georgi, Dieter. *Theocracy In Paul's Praxis and Theology*. Translated by David Green. Minneapolis: Fortress Press, 1991.

Hafemann, Scott. "The Glory and Veil of Moses in 2 Corinthians 3:7–14: An Example of Paul's Contextual Exegesis of the Old Testament." *Horizons in Biblical Theology 14, No. 1* (1992): 31–49.

Henry, Matthew. *Matthew Henry's Commentary on the Whole Bible*. Vol. 6 of *Acts to Revelation*. McLean, VA: MacDonald Publishing Company, 1985.

Hernando, James D. "2 Corinthians." *Full Life Bible Commentary to the New Testament*. Edited by F.L. Arrington and Roger Stronstad, 915–62. Grand Rapids: Zondervan, 1999.

Hill, Edmund. "Construction of Three Passages From St. Paul." *Catholic Biblical Quarterly 23.3* (1961): 296–301.

Kruse, Colin G. *New Testament Models for Ministry: Jesus and Paul*. Nashville: Thomas Nelson, 1985.

_____.*The Second Epistle of Paul to the Corinthians*. Grand Rapids: Eerdmans, 1987.

_____.*Paul, the Law, and Justification*. Peabody, MA: Hendrickson Publishers, 1997.

Lias, J.J., ed. *The Cambridge University Bible for Schools and Colleges: The Second Epistle to the Corinthians*. London: Cambridge University Press, 1897.

Lightner, Robert. "Theological Perspectives Theonomy; part 3: A Dispensational Response to Theonomy." *Bibliotheca Sacra vol.143* (1986): 228–45.

Martin, Ralph. *Word Biblical Commentary Vol. 40, 2 Corinthians*. Waco: Word, 1986.

Meyer, H.A.W. *A Critical and Exegetical Handbook to the Epistles to the Corinthians*. Tubingen, Germany: J.C.B. Mohr, 1987.

Moule, H.G.C. *The Second Epistle to the Corinthians: A Translation, Paraphrase, and Exposition*. Grand Rapids: Zondervan, 1962.

Plummer, Alfred. *A Critical and Exegetical Commentary on the Second Epistle of St. Paul to the Corinthians. 2nd ed*. Edinburgh: T&T Clark, 1915.

Propp, William H. "Did Moses Have Horns?" *Bible Review 4, no. 1* (1988): 30–37, 44.

Smalley, Stephen. *1, 2, 3 John*. World Biblical Commentary, vol. 51. Waco: Word, 1984.

Spencer A.B. *Paul's Literary Style: A Stylistic and Historical Comparison of II Corinthians 11:16–12: 13, Romans 8:9–39, and Philippians 3:2–4:13*. Jackson, MS: Evangelical Theology Society, 1984.

Stanley, Christopher D. *Paul and the Language of Scripture: Citation Technique the Pauline Epistles and Contemporary Literature*. Cambridge: Cambridge University Press, 1992.

Stockhausen, Carol K. "2 Corinthians 3 and the Principles of Pauline Exegesis." *Paul and the Scriptures of Israel*. Edited by Craig A. Evans and James Sanders, 165–86. Sheffield: JSOT Press, 1993.

Talbert, Charles Reading Corinthians: *A Literary and Theological Commentary on 1 and 2 Corinthians*. New York: Crossroad, 1987.

Tasker, R. V. G. *The Second Epistle of Paul to the Corinthians: An Introduction and Commentary*. Tyndale New Testament Commentary Series. Grand Rapids: Eerdmans, 1960.

Witherington, Ben. *Paul's Narrative Thought World: The Tapestry of Tragedy and Triumph*. Louisville: John Knox Press, 1994.

_____. *Conflict and Community in Corinth: A Social-Rhetorical Commentary on 1 and 2 Corinthians*. Grand Rapids: Eerdmans, 1995.

Young, Frances M. and David F. Ford. *Meaning and Truth in 2 Corinthians*. Grand Rapids: Eerdmans, 1988.

Greek Grammar Tools

BibleWorks. Version 4.0. Hermeneutika. Big Fork, MT. Software.

Brooks, James A. and Carlton L. Winbery. *Syntax of New Testament Greek*. Lanham, MD: University Press of America, 1979.

McKay, K. L. *A Syntax of the Verb in New Testament Greek: An Aspectual Approach*. New York: Peter Lang International Academic Publishing, 1994.

Dana, H. E. and Julius Mantey. *A Manual Grammar of the Greek New Testament*. Toronto: MacMillan Publishing, 1957.

Moule, C.F.D. *An Idiom Book of New Testament Greek*. Cambridge: Cambridge University Press, 1959.

Porter, Stanley E. *Idioms of the Greek New Testament*. 2nd ed. Sheffield: Sheffield Academic Press, 1994.

Robertson, A. T. *A Grammar of the Greek New Testament in the Light of Historical Research*. Nashville: Broadman Press, 1934.

Wallace, Daniel B. *Greek Grammar Beyond The Basics: Exegetical Syntax of the New Testament*. Grand Rapids: Zondervan, 1996.

Winbery, Carlton. Personal correspondence with author. November 13, 2001.

Zerwick, Maximilian. *Biblical Greek: Illustrated by Examples*. Rome: Pontifical Biblical Institute, 1953.

Textual Criticism

Aland, Kurt and Barbara. *The Text of the New Testament: An Introduction to the Critical Editions and to the Theory and Practice of Modern Textual Criticism*. 2nd ed. Translated by Erroll F. Rhodes. Grand Rapids: Eerdmans, 1989.

Metzger, Bruce M. *A Textual Commentary on the Greek New Testament*. 2nd ed. Stuttgart: United Bible Societies, 1998.

Translations/Versions

Septuaginta, Edited by Alfred Rahlfs. Stuttgart: United Bible Societies, 1979.

The Greek New Testament. 4th revised ed. Stuttgart: United Bible Societies, 1993.

Word Studies

Aalen, Sverre. "δόξα." *The New International Dictionary of New Testament Theology*. Edited by Colin Brown, 2:44–8. Grand Rapids, Zondervan, 1978.

Brandt, Theodor. "περισσεύω." *The New International Dictionary of New Testament Theology*. Edited by Colin Brown, 1: 728–31. Grand Rapids, Zondervan, 1978.

Brown, Colin and H. Seebass. "δικαιοσύνη." *The New International Dictionary of New Testament Theology*. Edited by Colin Brown, 3:352–77. Grand Rapids, Zondervan, 1978.

Danker, F.W. *A Greek-English Lexicon of the New Testament and Other Early Christian Literature*. 3rd ed. Chicago: University of Chicago Press, 2000.

Delling, G. "καταργέω." *Theological Dictionary of the New Testament*. Edited by Gerhard Kittel, I: 452–4. Grand Rapids: Eerdmans, 1964.

_____."ὑπερβάλλω." *Theological Dictionary of the New Testament*. Edited by Gerhard Kittel, VIII: 520. Grand Rapids: Eerdmans, 1964.

Kittel, Gerhard. "δόξα." *Theological Dictionary of the New Testament*, Edited by Gerhard Kittel, Π: 232–55. Grand Rapids: Eerdmans, 1964.

_____."κατάκρισις." In *Theological Dictionary of the New Testament*. Edited by Gerhard Kittel, ΙΠ: 951–2. Grand Rapids: Eerdmans, 1964.

Louw, Johannes P. and Eugene Nida. *Greek-English Lexicon of the New Testament: Based on Semantic Domains, Vol. 1*. New York: United Bible Societies, 1988.

Packer, J.I. "καταργέω," *The New International Dictionary of New Testament Theology*, Edited by Colin Brown, 1:73. Grand Rapids, Zondervan, 1978.

Schneider, Walter. "κατάκρισις." *The New International Dictionary of New Testament Theology*. Edited by Colin Brown, 2:362–67. Grand Rapids, Zondervan, 1978.

Spicq, Ceslas. "δόξα." *Theological Lexicon of the New Testament*. Edited by Ceslas Spicq, 1:362–79. Peabody, MA: Hendrickson, 1994.

_____."δικαιοσύνη." *Theological Lexicon of the New Testament*. Edited by Ceslas Spicq, 1:318–47. Peabody, MA: Hendrickson, 1994.

Turner, Nigel. *Christian Words*. Edinburgh: T&T Clark, 1980.

About the Author

A native of Carmel, Indiana, Keith Trump founded Living Truth Church (www.live-truth.org) in 2003. He continues to lead this thriving ministry. Prior to Living Truth, Keith ministered in churches throughout the United States as well as oversees in both Nicaragua and Haiti.

Keith has an overflowing passion for teaching the whole Word of God. The Lord took him through many years of preparation in order to accomplish this endeavor. In addition to graduating from Rhema Bible College, Keith holds baccalaureate degrees from Evangel University in both biblical studies and missions. He also has a master of divinity degree from Assemblies of God Theological Seminary.

While at Evangel, Keith earned multiple honors such as *Outstanding Greek Student*, the *Zondervan Medal of Achievement For Outstanding Greek Studies*, the *American Bible Society Scholars Award*, the highest distinction of Outstanding Biblical Studies Graduate, and many other scholarships. During his time at seminary, Keith received the prestigious Presidential Scholarship for each of his years of study.

In 2014, the Lord gave Keith the mandate to "Get my people into the language (Hebrew and Greek) of my Word!" In obedience to the that command, he launched the "Getting Greek"(www.gettinggreek. org) seminars. These seminars have taken off and begun taking believers out of the shallows of pop-Christianity and into the deeper water of God's Word. Throughout his ministry, Keith's greatest partner remains his wife of 24 years, Lori. Together, they have four children ranging in ages from 6 to 23. Keith's closest mentors include Rev. Tony Cooke and Pastor Rick Renner.

PRAYER OF SALVATION

God loves you — no matter who you are, no matter what your past. God loves you so much that He gave His one and only begotten Son for you. The Bible tells us that "... whoever believes in him shall not perish but have eternal life" (John 3:16 NIV). Jesus laid down His life and rose again so that we could spend eternity with Him and experience His absolute best on earth. If you would like to receive Jesus into your life, say the following prayer out loud and mean it in your heart.

Heavenly Father, I come to You admitting that I am a sinner. Right now, I choose to turn away from sin, and I ask You to cleanse me of all unrighteousness. I believe that Your Son, Jesus, died on the cross to take away my sins. I also believe that He rose again from the dead so that I might be forgiven of my sins and made righteous through faith in Him. I call upon the name of Jesus Christ to be the Savior and Lord of my life. Jesus, I choose to follow You and ask that You fill me with the power of the Holy Spirit. I declare that, right now, I am a child of God. I am free from sin and full of the righteousness of God. I am saved in Jesus's name. Amen.

If you prayed this prayer to receive Jesus Christ as your Savior for the first time, please contact us to receive a free book:

www.harrisonhouse.com
Harrison House
PO Box 35035
Tulsa, Oklahoma 74153

Getting Greek Seminars

For more information, to
watch our weekly webcast,
or to book a seminar in your
church or school,
visit www.gettinggreek.org

Fast. Easy. Convenient.

For the latest Harrison House product information and author news, look no further than your computer. All the details on our powerful, life-changing products are just a click away. New releases, email subscriptions, testimonies, monthly specials — find them all in one place. Visit harrisonhouse.com today!

harrisonhouse.com

The Harrison House Vision

Proclaiming the truth and the power

Of the Gospel of Jesus Christ

With excellence;

Challenging Christians to

Live victoriously,

Grow spiritually,

Know God intimately.